A MEMOIR

By Bernice (Bailey) Dietrich

and Melissa Bini

Copyright © 2023 Melissa Bini

All rights reserved.

ISBN-13: 979-8-218-20467-9

Lady Slippers

ACKNOWLEDGEMENTS

To her daughter, Carol, for organizing and deciphering years of hand-written journal entries.

To her grandson, Eric, for digitalizing over a dozen photo albums.

To my wife, Kaylan, for tolerating numerous rounds of edits.

DEDICATION

In Loving Memory of

Bernice Dietrich

1920-2022

Lady Slippers

Family Tree Early Years

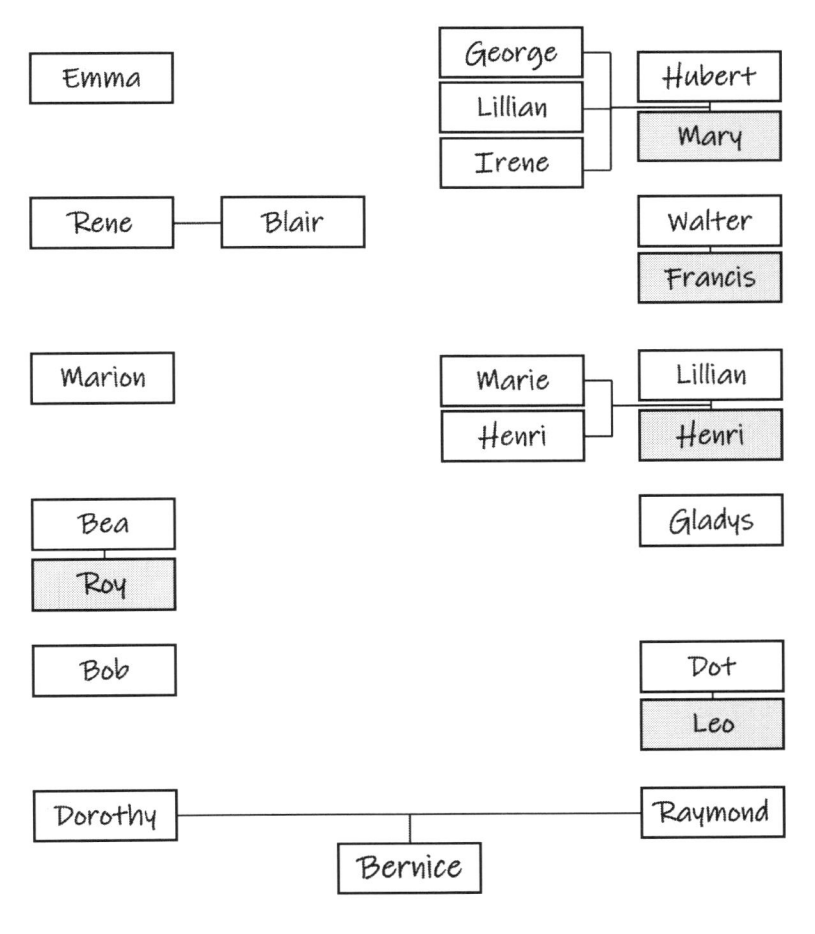

- Emma
- George / Lillian / Irene — Hubert / Mary
- Rene — Blair
- Walter / Francis
- Marion
- Marie / Henri — Lillian / Henri
- Bea / Roy
- Gladys
- Bob
- Dot / Leo
- Dorothy — Raymond
- Bernice

* Limited to family members mentioned.

5

Lady Slippers

FOREWORD

By Melissa Bernice (Dietrich) Bini

Bernice Dietrich, my grandmother, wanted to share her story with anyone who would listen. Whether it was a family member or the barista at Dunkin Donuts – she didn't care. She loved people and she loved to talk.

If you met her, the first thing she would clarify was the pronunciation of her name; it's Burn-us not BerNEEce. To make it easier, just think, rhymes with *furnace*.

Her memoir is bookended by Pandemics, as she grows up during the Great Depression and World War II. This firsthand account provides an intimate view of the Tri-State Area over a century of time. The world is changing; travel, medicine, modern enhancements, technology – most for the better. Her family suffers some harsh realities of the times and some unfortunate events.

She documented her story along the way. Her daughter, Carol, would later organize and type her entries up until 2007. When she passed in 2022, Carol and I picked up where she left off, adding some context for those unfamiliar with the area. As you read this, note her sense of humor, appreciation for life, stubbornness at times, and wanderlust. Maybe there's a hidden secret to living over 100 years.

CHAPTER 1

Dr. Smith

My life started in 1920, and almost ended at my birth. I was delivered by forceps, which took the skin off my left cheek and cut an opening above my right eyebrow. Because of my poor condition, I was baptized by the nurse in the old Staten Island Hospital (Smith Infirmary) on Castleton Avenue. Then, my life seemed threatened again when my mother was made aware that I was not receiving enough nourishment when she was nursing me. Her sister, Emma, a practical nurse, told mom that I was starving. Once I was started on formula in a bottle, I thrived.

My mother and father moved briefly to Saybrook, Connecticut where my father's family lived. Then it was back to Staten Island (New York) again. When I was about three, I lived on Victory Boulevard above Cannon Avenue. I was quite the handful to care for. It was there I decided the pet canary needed to take a bath. Somehow, I managed to grab the poor bird and washed him most thoroughly. He didn't survive! I almost got into trouble by dousing myself with a rather expensive ointment that was being used on me for impetigo. Guess I thought that if a little was good for me, all of it at once all over my whole body, including my hair, would make me better quicker.

At this location, my mother would let me outside to play on the sidewalk. Getting to know me better, she fastened me to the railing by a rope so I couldn't wander off or go into the street. My grandmother Ferguson lived on Meredith Avenue, so I often played in her fenced yard with my cousin Blair, who was 10 months older

Lady Slippers

than I. We decided Grandmother needed kindling wood for the kitchen stove. There was a chopping block in the backyard with an axe embedded in it, as was common practice at this time. Blair managed to pry the axe loose and I, ever helpful, held the wood for him. Next thing I knew I was running to Grandma with my right index finger hanging by a thread. Grandmother pushed the two ends of the finger together, wrapped it in a clean men's handkerchief and sent for Dr. Smith.

In his opinion, he thought the finger should have been removed. In Grandmother's opinion, the finger should have been sewn back on. She prevailed! Dr. Smith used five metal clips around that tiny finger. Afterwards, whenever he saw me, which became very often as I grew, he would say "Let me see that finger. You can really move it quite well." He was very proud of the way it healed, but Grandma and I knew it was *her* insistence that kept my finger on my hand that day.

The town I lived in, Travis, went under various names over the last hundred years or so. It was once known as Long Neck and then Linoleumville because of the factory at the end of Victory Boulevard.

My father started a business in Travis near Crabb's Lane. He had cars towed to his home, and from these cars, he made working models or sold parts salvaged from the wrecks of other cars. We lived in a small house consisting of four rooms. Then my Grandmother in Connecticut died. My Grandfather, my uncles Walter (Buster) and Hubert, my Aunt Gladys plus Teddy, the dog, all came to live with us. I started Kindergarten in P.S. 26.

Then we moved to a larger house on Vedder Avenue. Although the house was much larger, we were still crowded. Some of my mother's family were out of work because of the depression. Therefore, our home became their home until they could start over. At one time, 11 members of the combined family lived in a house with three bedrooms, an outhouse down the lane, two house dogs that couldn't stand the sight of each other, and one wild dog chained in the yard. The two house dogs, Teddy and Donnie, would not go anywhere near Walter, the wild one. To feed Walter, his dish had to be retrieved with a broom. The bowl was then filled and pushed back into his reach. He had a six-foot heavy chain, and he was so fast, he could catch and kill rats that lived nearby. He also managed to catch the neighbors' prized hens. He consumed the entire chicken, feathers, bones, and all. My dad felt sorry for him because it was so cold one winter day, so he put Walter inside the garage instead of under it. Walter showed his appreciation by tearing up the tire inner tubes, seats for cars, and anything else he could reach.

    My dad's junk yard was a great playground for us. The cars were dumped all around upside down on their roofs or sideways on their doors. We climbed in and out of them at will. One day in particular we chose a car that was lying on its passenger side. The other kids, being taller than I, had no problem letting themselves down into the driver's seat. I was short and needed some place to put a foot. I tried to get perched on the windshield, which was broken. Of course, my foot slipped and the broken windshield penetrated my right ankle. Once again, Dr. Smith was there to clamp me back together.

Another time, the game was "King of the Mountain". I lost the game and hit my head on a rock on the way down. Another visit by Dr. Smith and another clamp was put on my body. By this time, I was enrolled in P.S. 22 in Graniteville, Staten Island. There I encountered childhood diseases and had to sample them all as they came along, including scarlet fever, measles, chicken pox, whooping cough and ringworm. Dr. Smith made so many visits to our home, my dad used to say, "Every time I turn into the driveway, I meet him coming out!"

Did I mention that we had a brook in the back of the property? I regularly fell into said brook, by accident or design. Also, where the Bayonne Bridge[1] extension roadway is now, the area was always filled in with water. When it froze, we could slip and slide all the way up to Willowbrook Park.

My father found a new venture when he bought a fishing boat. The junk yard got sold and the boat replaced it. We moved to

---

[1] Bayonne Bridge connects Bayonne, New Jersey with Staten Island, New York. It was built in 1928-1931 according to Wikipedia.

Lady Slippers

Ruth Avenue. We had money. I was able to have dancing and piano lessons. Now I was in P.S. 30 in Westerleigh, Staten Island.

The money disappeared so we moved to Lake Avenue in Mariners Harbor. All the relatives, except one, had moved on with their lives. My grandfather had remarried. Gladys stayed with her father. Teddy, the dog, decided he liked the Vedder Avenue address and ran back there every time he could. Finally, the new owner said he wanted him to stay there so Teddy left us.

I remember the day that I had to enter the new school. Dad and Mom had to be at work, so I had to take myself up to P.S. 44[2] and enroll myself. I really didn't want to do this. It is not easy to enter a strange classroom with strange children staring at you. I do remember the kind Italian family across the street on Lake Avenue who invited me in and fed me pasta like one of their own. I didn't get into too much trouble there except to walk to school on the train tracks on top of the third rail which was covered by a wooden plank. I did place pennies on the track to see what would happen when the

---

[2] P.S. 44 also known as Thomas C. Brown School in Mariners Harbor, Staten Island.

train ran them over. My mother and I spent many days or evenings walking to the Port Richmond Library, the Empire Theater, and over the Bayonne Bridge to visit her sister, Emma. I was lined up on the approach to the Bayonne Bridge on the day that Franklin Roosevelt crossed it to visit[3]. Before that, we had a ferry from Port Richmond to Bayonne.

We left this location after a year and relocated on Wooley Avenue. This part of Wooley was a dead end with only one house beyond the one we lived. We had woods in front of us and fields and meadows where the street ended. It was mine to explore and I took full advantage of the environment. I climbed trees and swung on a rope from one tree to another. I waded in the brook, picked violets in the springtime, ice skated on the pond near Bradley Avenue (when there were no houses there at that time), and went sleigh riding down the hills that led to Victory Blvd. Of course, just plain sleigh riding was not exciting enough, so we would pour water on the sidewalks at

---

[3] Franklin D. Roosevelt's motorcade crossed the Bayonne Bridge on October 27, 1936, passing through the North Shore as part of his re-election campaign. Children were given the day off from school according to SILive.com.

Lady Slippers

night. Then we had an icy surface which made the ride much faster with no control at all over the steering. To stop before entering Victory Blvd. traffic, it was necessary to fall off the sled. It was also at this time that we used Waters Avenue in Westerleigh to slide down. To protect ourselves from cross street traffic, kids walking back up the hill would stop cars until the riders passed. That was a long ride down and a longer hike back up.

Summer days were spent at beaches on Staten Island. Midland Beach had a pool with a water slide. We had to pay to use this pool, so it was mostly out of bounds. We did use the beach. Our favorite beach was Bruggeman's in Huguenot. There was a big parking lot at the top of the cliff with a wooden staircase leading down to the beach. If you got there early in the day, you could use the picnic tables under the shade of trees that dotted the cliff and the beach. The remains of a long pier edged the property line. It was remnant of the days when excursion boats traveled from New York City proper to use the beaches and hotels of the South Shore of Staten Island. These beaches were clean and safe and nearby. The beach next to Bruggeman's was another favorite. This was also free, and we were able to buy soda and snacks in the lobby of the huge hotel. The remainder of the hotel had been destroyed by fire. The lobby survived and was a reminder of past glory days. It had a front lawn and tiled floors inside. The beach also had a pier way out into the bay to welcome visitors by boat. Our visits to the beach were family affairs. My mother's sister, Laurene had a car and transported us to these locations. Mom's other sister Aunt Beatrice also accompanied us on many occasions.

Faber Pool in Port Richmond was another place we gathered with our friends. We would walk to the pool in the mornings as it was free. Usually, we wore our bathing suits. We didn't like changing in an open area and there were few booths with doors. This pool was on the waterfront called the Kill Van Kull[4] across the river from Bayonne. It was equipped with diving boards, one of which was 15 feet high. I learned to first jump into the pool from that

---

[4] According to NYC Parks & Recreation website, Faber Pool opened in 1932 to provide an alternative to swimming in the dangerous, polluted water of the Kill Van Kull.

Lady Slippers

height and finally was able to do a swan dive without much form and grace, but without hurting myself. The pool had a center area which was 15 feet deep. This area has been removed[5] and no diving boards are now in the four city pools on Staten Island.

---

[5] According to NYC Parks & Recreation website, the pool went through restoration in 1996. A skate park was constructed in 2015.

CHAPTER 2

Chores & Outdoors

As my mother went on to a steady job, I was sent to Connecticut once school was out for the summer. After the last day of school, my Mom and Dad would drive me to South Lyme, Connecticut on the coast of Long Island Sound, just over the other side of the Connecticut River from Saybrook. This became another time of exploration and adventure. My Grandfather had remarried Catherine (Kitty). They were able to buy a four bedroom house on a 2 ½ acre plot of ground. To help pay the bills, they took in four sibling children from the state. They were paid for providing shelter, food, and clothing. These children were part of a larger family who were discovered living in a tent with their mother and father in the middle of winter under life threatening conditions. The children were two girls and two boys. When I stayed there, there were five of us to share the chores and the play times. The chores consisted of "slopping" the two pigs and herding the young turkeys into the sheltered area when it rained. The birds were too stupid to do this on their own. The animals also had to be fed twice a day as did the chickens and the cow. Eggs also had to be collected and brought to the house.

Another chore was delivering milk and eggs to customers who lived at the Mill Pond. These people made their own electric power by using a water wheel placed where the overflow from the pond on the way to the ocean turned the wheel. The path to this house led through cool, leafy woods. The problem was spiders. They would spin huge webs across the paths to ensnare flies and insects. None of us liked walking into their webs. It was the stuff of nightmares. You felt or sensed that along with the web strands you also managed to pick up a spider in your hair or clothes. Yech! Also, the pond property was guarded by a pair of domestic geese! As soon as you approached the property line, the geese attacked with enough noise to wake the dead. They used their beaks to latch onto your legs and twist the skin to make a nasty bruise. We tried to avoid contact with these guardians whenever we could.

Lady Slippers

Before we could go to the beach, my grandfather required each of us to pull a bushel basket of weeds from the vegetable garden, where he raised corn, lima beans, carrots, and beets.

We also went picking blueberries and huckleberries. There is nothing to compare with a ripe blueberry picked from the bush, warm with the sun and dirty as well. Many more found their way into our mouths as went into our pails. The ones we didn't eat were taken to a small roadside cafe on the street above ours. The owner bought all the berries we were able to bring to her and made fresh fruit pies with them. We got paid ten cents a pint. This we divided up among us and saved it. It was used to go to the movies in the nearby town on Saturday night. If we got lucky, we even had enough for all of us to have a five cent fudgesicle.

We had to be on the lookout for snakes. Staten Island didn't have poisonous snakes, but Connecticut did! They had rattlesnakes which sunned themselves on the rocks. There were other hazards as well. I remember one time while picking blueberries, Dorothy, the youngest member of our group, stepped on a nest of yellow jackets.

They swarmed all over her, but she was more concerned with the loss of her blueberries. She was afraid there'd be no movies for her. After rescuing her from the yellow jackets we put cooling mud on her bites. We proceeded to pick more berries so she would have enough to go to the movies and have a fudgesicle on Saturday.

The "overnight jar" was kept upstairs in the hallway. It was another chore for us kids. A week's duty was allotted to each of us. It would be quite heavy some mornings as six children and two adults relieved themselves in it during the nighttime hours. If you had a BM, it was the custom to wake your bedmate and stumble down the stairs, through the darkened household, out the side door to the outhouse, located a considerable distance from the house. Toilet paper consisted of whatever was at hand and mostly outdated Sears Roebuck or Montgomery Ward catalogs. They served a double usage during the day by providing you with reading material while you were sitting on the "throne".

I vividly remember one time when it was my turn to empty the chamber pot. I was barefoot, as was usual for all of us during the

Lady Slippers

summer. I had on long pants and caught my toe in my pants leg. I managed to catch the stair railing. However, the chamber pot spilled its entire contents down the stairs and into the dining room! I was given comforting looks along with many rags with which to soak up the urine first. Then I had to wash the entire staircase with warm soapy water to make sure no nasty smells lingered on. Remember we didn't have running water! A pump in the kitchen supplied water from a well in the side yard. Hot water was from water brought to a boil on the kitchen range. Showers were from well water brought from the well that was used to water the animals in the barn, the pigsty, the chicken coop, and the turkeys. Needless to say, *that* water was cold.

    The woods had many treasures including lady slippers. These were a beautiful type of wild orchid that were hidden in the wooded areas. My mother told me they used to be here on Staten Island also when she was growing up near where the Motor Vehicle Station is located off Victory Blvd. I wonder if any of them remain hidden here still.

On Sundays it was necessary for us all to get dressed and go to church. We walked up to the church barefooted, sat on the steps leading into the small wooden church, put on our shoes and went into the service. Then when we came out, we removed our shoes and walked home barefooted again. On the rare occasions that we went to New London, the nearest big town we also rode there barefoot. We put on our shoes when getting out on the streets of New London and then discarded the shoes as soon as possible on the ride home.

We spent our free time outside inventing pastimes. We knew that certain forms we found on milkweed plants contained a monarch chrysalis soon to hatch. Other forms hatched into praying mantises which fed on the plant destroying insects in our yards. Ugly caterpillars with horns ate the tomato plants almost overnight and wood ticks attached themselves to our bodies. We had to pluck them off and squash them. Tent caterpillars made nests in the wild cherry trees and ate the leaves. We gathered wild blackberries and the wild cherries and used them as food or made them into jams and jellies in the heat of summertime.

Lady Slippers

Living in the country setting like Travis or in Connecticut, chickens were bought through the mail. One hundred baby chicks would be delivered to our homes. They were taken out of the boxes as quickly as possible and given a mixture of foods and water. It was hoped that most of them would be hens. That would assure us of fresh eggs every day. Having too many roosters would lead to fights in the chicken yard, as one rooster strived to be in control of the whole hen flock.

To use a chicken for food, it first has to be killed. This usually meant its head had to be cut off. And yes, it is true; a chicken would run around for a while with its head cut off just as the expression says. The dead chicken had to be immersed in boiling water which released a very unpleasant smell, one not easily forgotten. All the feathers would become loosened from the skin and then plucked out. If new pillows were needed, these feathers could then be washed, dried in the sun and then stuffed into special material calling "ticking". The chickens' bodies then had to be cut opened and the insides removed. The heart, liver and giblets were used to make gravy. The rest was used to make Sunday dinner. For many of the families, the carcass was used to make chicken soup, another important part of our diet. It seemed there was always a pot of soup bubbling on the kitchen stove, either chicken or beef. Beef soup was made from big bones that the butcher would give you for free.

Living on Staten Island when I was young was a place of freedom and exploration. We were able to roam about the brooks, ponds, and woods in safety, even when alone, no matter what part of the island we lived on. Our doors were never locked at night while we were at home. Even our dogs were free to roam the area. We rode our bikes if we were fortunate enough to have them. Mine was a recycled one. One wheel was from one bike, the other from a second one, with no fenders and no brakes. To stop the bike, I either had to fall off or stick my shoe into the fork of the bike where the wheel passed. The tire had to be pumped up every time the bike was ridden, but I enjoyed the ride whenever I could coax the bike to cooperate.

Lady Slippers

CHAPTER 3

High School Sweethearts

When I attended P.S. 30, there were no school buses available and no rides from mom or dad. So, I had to hike to school regardless of the weather. When I graduated from P.S. 30, Port Richmond High School was next. At that time, I was given 10 cents a day for carfare. A bus on Victory Blvd would take me to Meiers Corners to transfer to the Jewett Avenue line. I'd walk the rest of the way from Port Richmond proper to the high school. The fare was 5 cents one way. Most times, I walked all the way. Then I could use the money for a candy bar, a treasured treat. Moving from Wooley Ave to Travis, the bus became the only way to go, as it was then too far to walk. The bus took us to Bulls Head, where we transferred to the Richmond Avenue bus.

It was in this time period that I met Henry Dietrich. He lived in Travis most of his life, having been born in McNamara's farmhouse just off Victory Blvd near the cannon monument[6]. His family returned to Germany when he as nine months old. They lived there for a while and his sister, Leah attended school there for a while. Henry developed pneumonia while on board the ship. He was so very ill that he almost died! His family stayed in Germany but when the country went bankrupt, they lost their home. They managed to scrape together enough cash to buy their passage back to the US. Max Dietrich went to work at the linoleum factory in Travis. They bought a home on Cannon Avenue, one of the many Decker

---

[6] Corner of Victory Blvd and Cannon Ave.

family houses[7] on Staten Island. It was then well over 100 years old. The original part of the house had outer walls lined with brick as insulation. The house consisted of one huge living room and one low ceilinged attic room. The living room's one outside wall had a fireplace. The fireplace chimney extended to the attic room where there was another fireplace. It had tiny windows in the front. Another room was added which made it a three-room house. Once the Dietrichs moved into it, an extension was put on the back. It had three small bedrooms on one side and a kitchen and bath on the other with a back lobby and a side door. The roof was raised, adding larger windows in the front, a bathroom, living room with a step down to a kitchen and bedroom. There was a hall and staircase that completed a three-room apartment upstairs which was rented out. This became Henry's home until he married. He was joined by another sister Anna and a brother Edmund (another baby Mary died on or after one of the crossings from Germany).

---

[7] The Decker Family owned Decker Farm (ca. 1810). It remains NYC's oldest working family style farms according to historicrichmondtown.org. It became a NYC landmark in 1967.

The family was enlarged by a boarder from time to time. Friends from Germany wanted to come here to live. At that time, a person wishing to emigrate here had to be "sponsored" by a family who was gainfully employed. This sponsor promised to house and feed the newcomer until he found a job to support himself in this country. Finding work here was not easy because the country was in the big "Depression".

Henry's father, Max worked at the linoleum factory as did my grandfather from my mother's family, Joseph Ferguson. Max was injured at work. The linoleum was a very heavy quality flooring made from canvas backing and various resins. It was called "battleship" linoleum. Max's job was to roll up the finished product so it could be shipped out. One day, he got his right arm caught in the roller. It was so badly mangled that the bone in the arm had to be replaced with metal. The company promised him a job for the rest of his life as compensation. He became a watchman at the plant. This was not bad until the plant went out of business. Their product was so durable it never had to be replaced. Max now had to find a job he could do as disabled as he was. He became an exterminator at Seaview Hospital.

My grandfather, Joseph was not so fortunate. He was hit in the neck by the product. This led him to develop cancer which grew into his throat and choked him to death at the age of 50[8].

Henry's mother did her part by cleaning other people's homes besides taking care of her own. Edmund died at the age of 11, of some common illness.

Henry and I went on our first date when we were about 17. The Protestant churches on this side of Staten Island used to band together once a year and rent an excursion boat for a cruise. It started at a dock in Mariners Harbor and went across New York Harbor up the East River to Rye Beach Park. There people could swim at the beach or spend the day at the amusement park. All would come home sunburned and exhausted after trying to pack in every new experience into one day – the rides, the food, the beach, and the sail

---

[8] No family medical records have been found to verify this diagnosis.

over the water. Both of us nearly had disasters because neither of us wanted to tell the other we had to use the bathroom!

We then spent another day at the World's Fair[9] in Flushing Meadows in 1939. That day we traveled by public transportation from Travis and went by bus, ferry boat and subway. We tried to see every exhibit there. We stayed until closing time, returning by subway, ferry and bus and barely awake by that time. We arrived at Four Corners only to realize we missed the last bus of the night home for Travis. There was only one thing to do – start walking! Our feet and legs protested every step of the way. At that time, I was living in the last house in Travis on Wilde Ave. Henry was at the other end on Cannon. He had to walk me home and then walk back to his house (another mile or so). Meanwhile my mother was very worried. We had no telephone to call her and tell her we were okay, and she had no way to receive our call as we didn't have a phone in the house. What a courtship memory.

---

[9] New York World's Fair was the second most expensive American world's fair of all time. Many countries around the world participated and over 44 million people attended in two seasons from 1939 to 1940 according to Wikipedia.

Lady Slippers

One time we were wandering around at the end of Victory Blvd. There were abandoned buildings there from the days before the Goethals Bridge put the ferries to New Jersey out of business. There was also a historical marker there on the left side of the roadway with a bronze plaque noting that this was the Blazing Star Ferry Crossing dating the Stagecoach era[10]. The bronze plate had been removed years ago by people who recycled the metal for a few dollars. This day was a Sunday. As we passed the time in this desolate unused place (only the buses and a few cars used it to turn around), Henry found a five dollar bill. We hurried to my house, left a note for my mom telling her of our good fortune and that we were on our way to New York City to see a show at Radio City Music Hall. At that time, you could see a short stage show, a movie and a cartoon show or serial like "The Perils of Pauline"[11] and have lunch nearby at an all the spaghetti you could eat or a Horn & Hardart

---

[10] A stagecoach is a large, closed horse-drawn vehicle formally used to carry passengers and often mail along a regular route between two places. Reference Oxford Dictionary.
[11] A 1914 American melodrama film serial according to Wikipedia.

Restaurant[12]. This eating place featured sandwiches behind little glass doors. People behind the glass would keep the windows refilled as food was taken out. It was a precursor of the vending machine. It also had desserts like apple pie, Jell-o, cake, or custard. You put your coin in the slot, the door opened, and the food was yours. It was automation at its best. Bus fare and ferry fare was five cents a ride. Many times, we walked down to the ferry from Radio City on 6th Avenue and 50th Street. We would revel in the sights, sounds and smells of the ever moving city, the city that never sleeps.

Henry bought his first car around this time. It was an old two-seater Chevy. He learned to drive it by trial and error. He'd get in it and try to shift it into gear once he was able to start the engine. One foot let the clutch out and then the car lumbered into motion. One day the car went into reverse instead of first. It backed into the neighbor's fence. Henry had to quickly replace the fence to fend off the man's anger *and* his father's anger besides, for causing this

---

[12] Chain of cafeterias in New York City and Philadelphia opened by John V. Horn and Frank Hardart, where low priced prepared food and beverages were obtained, especially from coin-operated compartments. Reference Britannica.com/topic/Horn-and-Hardart-Automat

disruption in the neighborhood. The engine of the car was very tricky. Usually, my dad would have to tinker with it and curse it a bit. Then it would spring to life. Both Henry and I learned to drive on the quiet streets of Travis. The furthest it ever went was to Bulls Head to the gas station there. The gas was five gallons for a dollar. The one day I was driving, I attempted to make a right turn off Victory Blvd, but the Chevy decided not to cooperate. It refused to make right turns. I was able to stop after mounting the sidewalk but not hitting people or the building. It was quite a chore to get the car back home again without making any right turns. The car cost ten dollars and was sold "as is" for ten dollars. It was a learning experience for both of us.

The house we lived in on Wilde Avenue (the last house in Travis) had been the factory house for the superintendent of the factory. It was a big house with very high ceilings and lots of property around it. During the days when the factory was operating, it was heated by furnaces in the factory, which supplied steam heat to the radiators in the house. It also supplied hot water to this house.

We did have a bathroom upstairs with one of the first bathtubs in town. It was a huge tub made of cast iron and painted whenever it needed the job. It was set in wainscoting to support it. Of course, by the time we lived in this house, the water pipes were corroded. You turned on the water upstairs, went downstairs and did a few chores and maybe when you returned upstairs, you had enough water to sit in and wash. You didn't do this in the wintertime. It was too cold in there then.

The house has a kitchen big enough to drive your car into. It had a place to put coal on with a little door to fill up the bucket. It had built in closets on the side with coal, another closet built into the inside wall with room for a huge range, a sink, table, and chairs. The range was converted to a kerosene range used for cooking and heating. I say "heating" with tongue in cheek. We had a goldfish we won at an amusement park. It was kept near the sink area about three feet from the range. One night poor goldfish froze to death in his bowl with the glass broken by the ice!

Lady Slippers

The lovely cabinets in the kitchen had all been invaded by rats looking for food. They would gnaw their way into the rooms where the piping from the factory came in. They made holes in the back of drawers. Our cat wouldn't go after these rats. It was afraid of them. They were bigger than he was. One night after Henry and I had been married, we were awakened by this knocking noise. It finally stopped. In the daylight hours, we found our room had been invaded by one of the rats. He had taken an apple from a basket of apples we had picked. He had been trying to get the apple through the door, but it wouldn't go through the opening. He had eaten as much of it as he could before he abandoned it.

We had a potbelly stove in the dining room. When you had a roaring fire in this stove and its belly was cherry red, you were able to sit near the stove. One side near the stove would be toasty warm while the other side was cold. The living room remained closed off with doors that slid into the walls. Both living room and dining room has beautiful bay windows. The living room also had full length windows which opened onto a covered porch. This was very refreshing in the summertime (if you could manage to keep the mosquitoes out while letting the cool breeze in). My bike was kept in the kitchen. One day my dad mounted the bike, rode it through the kitchen, back bedroom, and dining room and into the living room to get his cigar which he had left there.

Henry dug up a huge area on the side of the house for a garden. The wildlife outside loved this. The birds got the bean plants as soon as they poked through the dirt. The wild rabbits ate the lettuce plants and the tops of carrots. Henry had to erect a solid wooden plank fence around the garden to protect the produce.

Washing clothes at this time was an all-day job. You started by putting all the white laundry into an oval shaped pot that covered two burners of the range in the kitchen. You filled the pot with water and lye soap and then you boiled the laundry for several hours. You then transferred the steaming clothes to a laundry tub and scrubbed them over a washboard. Both jobs were very tiring and hand wrecking tasks. Then the clothes had to be rinsed out in clean water to remove the strong lye soap. You took these sheets and blouses and

Lady Slippers

wrung them out with the strength of your wrists to expel as much moisture as possible. Then you took your basket of wet clothes out into the yard and pinned them onto a clothesline with wooden clothes pins. In the wintertime, the sheets would freeze into one solid icy mass. It would take all of your strength to pry the clothespins off the line and the sheet. Somehow you had to get through the door and drape the frozen objects over chairs to dry them. If you wanted to be considered a "good housekeeper" you had to iron the bed clothes. Otherwise, you slept on much wrinkled sheets and pillow cases. Sometimes you put up lines in your kitchen to eliminate this hassle. Better yet, if you have an unused attic, you hung clothes up there. I have heard that even the White House had one room in which to hang clothes to dry. Every Monday wash would be hung out to dry and every Tuesday it would be the day to iron it. Pulley lines were used in upstairs apartments to take advantage of the breezes. In nice weather, the clothes would smell like all outdoors. You wanted to put the clothes on as soon as they dried because they smelled so good.

Henry and I spent many lazy days riding our bikes. We rode up to Richmond Avenue to Arthur Kill Road. There were streets and sidewalks off Arthur Kill Road that had been abandoned by the builders. There were few cars and fewer trucks to contend with as a bike rider. There were many truck farms on Staten Island on Richmond Avenue and in Travis. Travis had three – Molenhoffs was a large one with a greenhouse, Wegmans had a smaller farm and there was another small one on Victory Blvd across from Wegmans. There was also one near Travis Ave and Richmond as well as one on Travis Avenue where the Bird Sanctuary is now and a large one where the mall is. These farms grew lettuce, carrots, beets, beans, tomatoes, and Swiss chard. These crops were harvested and sent on trucks into New York City by ferry to feed the people "fresh farm products". Henry worked on the farm from the time he was eleven until he finished high school. The hours were from six to six every day including Saturday. The pay was a dollar a day. The work included digging, planting, weeding, and harvesting. A side product was a handful of arrowheads as some of the farms had been dug over

Lady Slippers

an old Indian burial ground. When Henry was older, he was sent by truck to the Armory on Manor Road. They had horses there and the manure had to be shoveled from the stalls there onto the truck and then taken to the farm where it was spread on the fields. The greenhouses were used to get the seeds started early in the spring to later be transplanted into the fields as the weather warmed up. Flowers were also grown in the greenhouses for Easter, Thanksgiving and Christmas. Henry also sold Liberty magazines[13] to various homes in the area. He was recycling long before laws went into effect mandating it. He brought home copper wire, iron scrap metal and pots and pans. A man used to come around with a wagon every so often. He would weigh the different metals and pay a certain amount which was different for each metal, copper being worth the most. With this salvage money of his, Henry was able to buy his bike. This helped him get to whichever farms he was working at and to deliver his magazines. Most of the money he earned at the farm had to be turned over to his mother which was the

---

[13] Liberty magazines were an American weekly general interest magazine originally priced at 5 cents according to Wikipedia.

custom of the European families that came here to live. The boys worked at the farms and the young girls did the housework for families that needed it done in their homes.

My mother had a group of friends who she had known since her childhood growing up in Travis. She and her sisters and these friends would gather in Jessie's house once a month. Jessie and her husband, Dick, lived in a large house on property now owned by Con Edison off Victory Blvd. The house sat back quite a bit from the road. It had a large dining room, a living room, a library room, and a large old-fashioned kitchen. The library had a huge table in it like one that is used in conference rooms with many chairs around it. We would all sit around that table and play bingo for pennies. Then we would go into the dining room. This would be loaded with food. Each family that visited brought a covered dish with them. Jessie would supply the cakes and pies. When I say each family, I mean the babies were bundled up for the visit and then played around on the floor or sat at the table if they were older. Music would be playing in the living room and those who wanted could dance in there. The men would gather to talk among themselves. It was a way to visit, have a few laughs and talk with friends. It didn't cost much money for anyone and mixed all the generations together.

Jessie's yard was bordered on one side by an athletic field. Travis had its own baseball team and a soccer team called "The Favorites". This team won many games on the island and once held first place in its league. We could sit on high seats in Jessie's yard and watch these games.

When my mother ended up in the hospital with appendicitis, I stayed at Jessie's house. My mother was very ill after her operation with peritonitis[14]. It took three weeks for her to pull through this. At the same time, Henry's mom, Stefania, was in the same hospital after a kidney operation that brought her close to death. Henry and I were taking Regents (state tests) in our high school, but we managed to get through these challenging tests and visit our moms almost every day. It was a worrisome time for us both.

---

[14] Inflammation of the peritoneum, typically caused by bacterial infection either via the blood or after rupture of an abdominal organ. Reference: Oxford Dictionary.

Henry was ahead of me in school, so he graduated six months before I did. Then we went out looking for our first jobs. This was still Depression time in 1938 and 1939. There were no jobs unless you had experience. We made many trips to the city and filled out many applications every day. Places on Staten Island like Proctor & Gambles in Mariners Harbor just shook their heads when we came to their offices. Downtown New York, with so many offices was the same. Even using an employment agency did not get us a job.

I finally got a job here on Staten Island in a Real Estate Office. Henry got a job in nearby New Jersey at American Cyanamid Factory. He had to take a small boat over there every day. The boat was run by an enterprising fellow from Travis. He ferried the workers back and forth from a small dock at the end of Cannon Avenue. Henry ended up doing shift work unloading sulfur from the ships and cleaning resin deposits from the inside of tanks. The job exposed him to dangerous chemicals including those that leaked from pipes. It ate holes in their clothing, and they had to breathe noxious odors. But at least he had a job, and we could plan to marry.

Lady Slippers

My job was to type and keep the books for the Real Estate Office and a towing company. I also had to answer the phone, sweep up the office every day and clean the bathrooms. Plus, on occasion, I showed apartments to prospective renters. I stayed with this job for one year, got the "experience" wanted by all those offices in New York City and tried my luck in the city once more. I was successful this time. I typed insurance policies for people buying autos on credit. Now we had enough money to get married.

CHAPTER 4

The Falls & The Draft

We tied the knot on September 28, 1941, at St. Anthony's Church in Travis with my friend Ann and Henry's friend Walter standing up for us. We followed the ceremony with the four of us traveling to the city for dinner on the town. Walter and Ann returned home while Henry and I spent our first night together in a hotel in the city. The following day we took the train to Buffalo and then to Niagara Falls. We spent one night in a hotel in that city, but it was too noisy for us. The walls seemed to be made of paper and we could hear everything going on in the adjoining room. We were afraid to move. If we could hear the neighbors in their room, then we were sure they could hear us. We looked for another room in the morning and found one in an old, converted mansion. This home had windows in the front that were curved into a bow shape. The panes of glass were also bow shaped. We then proceeded to explore the entire area. We went down to the walkway that took you below the American Falls. It was made of wood and was very slippery. We had two don rubber coats and pants to keep us dry. We rode on the boat that went almost under the Canadian Falls and saw the falls lit up at night. We heard the story of a fellow who went over the falls in a barrel. We even got to examine the barrel itself. All good things have to come to an end, and we had to return home. Three months later, Pearl Harbor[15] was attacked. Our lives changed drastically. For four

---

[15] December 7, 1941

years, we had to endure separate lives under great stress, except for some stolen moments when Henry had a three day pass.

As I mentioned above, 1941 was a memorable year for me and my husband, Henry. We had survived twenty years of the Great Depression. It was a time when food, clothing and housing were hard to come by. When your shoes had holes in them, you went to the 5 & 10 cent store and bought soles which you glued into your shoes, if you had the dollar it cost. If you didn't have the money, you cut inner soles from old cardboard boxes and inserted them into your shoes. This worked fine unless it rained. Then they became a soggy mess. Sometimes, the paper came loose and flapped nosily as you walked. It was very annoying and embarrassing although almost everyone had the same problem.

Frankfurters and beans, soup made from bones the butcher gave you, or if you were lucky a ham bone, was a common meal. Soup included broth from the meat bones or chicken, celery, onions, and leftovers from a previous meal. Refrigeration consisted of a 25 cent block of ice that the iceman delivered to your home each day.

He carried it into your house using ice tongs. It went into the top of your ice box where it kept your food cold. You had to remember to empty the tray under the ice box every day or you had a flood on the kitchen floor as the ice melted.

If your family was fortunate enough to have a house to live in, when tragedy overcame other family members, you took them in, housed them and shared your food with them. You also shared your bed with them and the bed bugs that infested most every older home. To keep the bed bug population down, you doused the bed frame and springs in kerosene. Of course, they were also under the wallpaper in the rooms of the house. Roaches were also all over. This was before the days of DDT spray[16] for control of pests.

People worked from six to six for $1 a day either doing back breaking work on a farm or housework. To get a job after high school meant traveling from one factory or office to another to put in applications. The answer was always the same. If you had no

---

[16] DDT (dichloro-diphenyl-trichloroethane) was developed as the first modern synthetic insecticides in the 1940s according to the United States Environmental Protective Agency (www.epa.gov)

Lady Slippers

experience with the job force, you were not considered at all. It helped if you knew somebody in the office or factory who would speak up for your reliability or character.

This was the situation we had lived in for the first twenty years of our lives. So, you can understand our great joy and happiness when we were able to travel by train to Niagara Falls for a few days on our honeymoon. The train trip was a great adventure in itself, a dream come true. We had spent almost four years of dating since we had met in high school. Our dates were mainly bicycle rides on the country streets of Staten Island, a movie once a month where you saw two shows and, if you went on a certain day; you might get a dinner plate or cup and saucer. All of this cost less than 25 cents each.

You must remember we did not have televisions or computers in our homes at this time. Few of our neighbors had phones in their houses. So many things have come about in our lifetime, I cannot mention them all, but they include: Bic pens, paper clips, zippers, Velcro, air conditioners and roller blades, just to name a few.

We had had a carefree time in Niagara Falls until we received word from my mother that while we were enjoying ourselves Henry had received his draft notice! Our government was worried about the events taking place in Europe between Germany & Italy and France & England and had instituted a draft into the services. This notice shattered our world and brought us home with trepidation as to our future lives. Would everything come to an end just at the beginning of our marriage? We faced an uneasy future indeed. The worst part of it was not knowing what was before us. We thought of the worst things such as being apart from each other, him being sent away for military service and the unthinkable, him not coming home again. Tears and fears filled our days and nights. Once he was sent away, we spent our spare time writing letters to each other and waiting for those letters to be answered and delivered back to us. Many other couples in the same situation did not survive the separation. Many other husbands did not return after the war started. The training these men underwent was fraught with problems. The US did not have enough supplies to use for this many men in the early days of our mobilization. Rifles had to be shared by many men. Stove pipes were used in place of bazookas for practice. Henry ended up in Anniston, Alabama for further training.

After being apart for many months, I decided to visit him over a weekend. I left right from work in New York City, went to Pennsylvania Station and took my first solo train ride. The train took me to Atlanta, Georgia. There I had to change trains to get the one to Alabama. This meant changing to another train line at another station. The train to Anniston was on a single rail track. It had to go into a siding to wait for another train going in the other direction. The train I was riding in was from another time period. It had a coal burning engine with smoke pouring from its stack along the right of way. All the windows were opened to take advantage of any breeze stirred up by our passage. Of course, this let in the smoke and embers from the smokestack. The train was crowded with young men in uniform. I was the object of all their eyes as there were no young or old women traveling on the trains. It was a very long, bone wearying trip. When I finally arrived at Anniston Station on that hot Saturday, I was filled with anticipation. I was about to see my husband BUT he wasn't at the station! "What do I do now?" I wondered. I hesitated only a few minutes. I found a phone and called the base commander. I told him that I had arrived to visit my husband. He then informed me that my husband had been transferred to Fort Bragg, North Carolina on the day that I had left New York City. What a predicament!

I re-boarded "the train". I say "the train" because I felt it to be a nightmare ride. It was only to be endured because it was to bring me to Henry for a few hours. Now it was to take me away from my happy anticipation into frustration and uncertainty. Arriving back in Atlanta, Georgia, hot, sticky, and covered with sooty streaks on my face, arms, and clothes, I went to the window to speak to a person manning the desk. I explained that I did not want to return to New York on the route I came in on. Instead, I asked them to re-route me through Fayetteville, North Carolina. I was still hoping that

Lady Slippers

I could at least see Henry. In those days train tickets came in segments, each for a different portion of each rail line. Rail lines in the US used the same tracks but each state had its own owners and lines. Tickets from one section to another were collected by the conductors as you passed over their section. The clerk said that this new ticketing couldn't be done. I stormed over to the USO desk which was common to all train stations and there told my sad story to them. The USO had volunteers all over the country trying to help the armed forces and civilians iron out all the problems that comes about under adverse conditions. These people walked me back to the ticket window and said, "Sign this ticket transfer now!" It was done. I spent another night on a train crowded with armed forced of all kinds. One woman was traveling with her wedding dress. As soon as she reached her man, they were to be married before he was sent overseas to fight in this long and bloody war.

      Upon reaching Fayetteville, I disembarked with my suitcase at the station. I made another call to the army based and explained my situation. I was told that Henry's entire unit was confined to base for a few days. Once again, my hopes were dashed. After this marathon train ride from New York City to Atlanta, Georgia to Anniston, Alabama to Atlanta, Georgia to Fayetteville, North Carolina all without the use of a shower or change of clothes, I was frustrated once more. However, my fears were not realized this time. My husband was given a special pass! It took about an hour to see him coming toward me in uniform. He was as excited to see me as I was to see him. He did get a dressing down from the unit commander for allowing me to travel that far under the existing conditions at that time. We found a hotel room for our few hours together. It was hard to know which was more welcome. Being together again in privacy or the cooling showers we shared. The change of clothes helped too.

    All too soon, it was time to take the train back to New York City at night. This time was more interesting as I had no seat at all! After traveling all Friday night and all day and night Saturday, I spent Sunday night sitting on my suitcase! I arrived about 8AM on Monday morning at Penn Station. I went to my office job, went into

Lady Slippers

the bathroom there where I washed up, changed my clothes, and spent the day typing up auto insurance policies. When I got back to Travis that Monday night, my mother met me with a sad face and said, "You didn't get to see him, did you?" He had sent telegrams to me on Friday telling me about the impending move. One went to my home and then he tried to reach me on the train at Washington, DC. The odyssey came to a successful ending with me telling my mother, "Oh, yes, I did so get to see him." She was amazed that at the age of 21, I had managed to overcome all of those obstacles that fate threw at me and completed my mission. I was reunited with my mate at least for a few hours.

That was the first visit during war time. We tried to be together on three day passes as often as time and money allowed us. One time when I traveled by bus or train, I was informed that the Potomac River was in a flood stage[17] so no trains were being allowed over it. In fact, empty freight trains were put on the bridge to try and

---

[17] According to History.com the Potomac River flooded in October 1942 from heavy rainfall likely related to a southern tropical storm. 800 soldiers and 300 civilians packed sandbags to build a barrier in attempts to protect the White House.

add weight to it to keep it in place. What to do now! I made my way to the bus depot, fought for a seat on a bus traveling south using a bridge that was high above the flooded river. I finally made it to Fayetteville and once again Henry was not there to meet me. He was waiting for me at the train station several blocks away. I had no way to tell him of the change of plans (today's cell phones would have been handy!).

While I was fighting travel battles, Henry was trying to find a place for us to stay without using all of his available money. When he was inducted into the army, his paycheck was $21 a month. He had to pay for the cleaning of his uniforms, razor blades, shaving cream, plus postage to send his letters to me and his family. Later on the pay went up and postage for the servicemen became free.

One room we stayed in was so small you had to step over the bed to get in or out of the room. The other room was a huge one in an old mansion. It had a potbelly stove in it to keep it warm in the winter. This time in history was before the advent of central heating in most homes. Of course, to use the stove you had to have something to burn in it. We found out the hard way what the former tenant had used! We went to the bed and ended up with a crash onto the floor. The downstairs tenant came rushing upstairs in a panic to find us picking ourselves up off the floor. It seems the fuel for the stove was the wooden slats that were supposed to support the springs and mattress of the bed!

We also stayed at the USO which was conveniently located across from the train station, and it was cheap. There were two beds in a room, and we shared a bath with the room on the other side. We found that this facility was an adventure in itself. First, the mattresses were so thin and worn you ended up in the middle of the bed regardless of where your body started out. You just sort of slid to the center. Sweat poured off you as there were no fans or air conditioners. When the train came, the locomotive had to blow the whistle at every road crossing to warn of its approach. The building shook with every turn of the engine's wheels and at night the headlight of the train bathed the room with its light as it approached.

You had no doubt it was coming from the frequent sound, light and motion shows.

One of the good things about this town was the ice cream soda we found there. They were huge drinks and so refreshing. We named them "Awful awfuls" and they were better than lunch. One of the bad things was the fact that the water fountains, bathrooms and eating places were segregated. Coming from New York City, this was not our usual practice. If we boarded a bus here, we were not allowed to sit in the back and the Negroes were not allowed to sit in the front. We could not join them at a table even though we wanted to sit with them. For many southerners, it was as if the Civil War has never been fought.

I wanted to stay in town but there were no jobs available for me. The stores in the area, the five and dime, and the restaurants had a policy of only hiring their own residents – they really didn't like us "Yankees". I could have picked cotton in the fields, but I didn't think I would last long at that job. It paid the princely sum of $1 for 100 pounds. The cotton plant is rather short in height so you must bend over. The individual cotton bolls weigh almost nothing when picked. So, cotton plucking was not an option for me, I couldn't stand being out in the blazing sun with biting bugs, it was too much of a back breaking job.

We finally found a solution. Henry would come up to Washington D.C. He could hitchhike in his uniform and most every trucker would pick him up. I would meet him at the train or bus station. We would walk around the capital and explore the city. We could enjoy some time together as often as we could.

My uncle spent most of his four war years in the Pacific. He contracted "jungle rot"[18] and he never completely got rid of it for the rest of his life. My cousin served in the Pacific as a Seabee. The Seabees were a branch of the Navy. They built airports, bases for the arm, bridges and roads where jungle islands were before.

This time was very hard on many marriages. The women didn't have the companionship they expected. They sometimes had

---

[18] Also known as "trench foot" according to Wikipedia. A chronic tropical ulcer, that formed when feet were exposed to water for extended periods, like marshes or wet boots.

children with no help, either money wise or having a father present. Daddy was a picture on the mantle. Baby was a picture in his wallet – not a child he got to hold or cuddle. Four years was a long time to live on memories alone.

Several times during the war, Henry was packed up and ready to leave. These times coincided with events in Europe. During the D-Day invasion[19], many of the airborne troops and glider crews, such as his, were lost in combat. The Germans had anticipated the gliders' arrival and erected cement columns in every large empty field. The gliders would hit the pillars and break up or go on fire, so losses were very high. The two man crew and its cargo were destroyed. The vols were "sitting ducks" as they floated down to earth. Marksmen could pick them off and trees ensnared them in their branches. A row of bullets into a glider could cause it to burst into flames. Therefore, replacements were needed after every engagement. When Italy was invaded, "friendly fire" took out the unit. Mistaken information was given to the army on the ground who

---

[19] June 6, 1944

Lady Slippers

thought a German unit was attacking. Each time Henry was about to be deployed he was returned to his unit in Fort Bragg and assigned to instruct the new recruits.

Our visits during the war came to an end in June of 1943 with the premature birth of our first child, Carol. This led to a whole new chapter of our life – one as parents. Carol was born early because I developed a problem with my kidneys. The infection had to be brought to a halt as it threatened both of our lives. Toxic material was spilling into my body. The treatment consisted of flushing out the kidneys. This resulted in the premature birth. I was in labor off and on from Friday until the following Tuesday. Carol weighed in at a little over 4 pounds. She was kept in the hospital until she weighed 6 pounds. My doctor wanted her on mother's milk for its health benefits. This meant I had to expel the milk from my breasts daily and then take it to the hospital by bus. From Travis, where we lived at the time, a bus would take me to Richmond Ave, where I could transfer to a bus at Port Richmond. Then I would go as far as Castleton Ave and transfer to the Castleton Ave bus. Because it was still wartime, we had no car available. It was also a hot and humid summer. This lasted for a full month. Carol thrived on the breast milk and survived the dangers of the incubators. Many babies received pure oxygen for breathing over a long period of time had their eyesight destroyed[20]. Later little eyes were protected while inside the incubators.

 We delayed having Carol baptized until her daddy could be home. Getting home for her birth had been a nasty problem. Henry was frantic with worry and concern about the two of us. He managed to get an emergency pass but had no money for the train or bus fare. The Red Cross would not give him the money, a mere $20 or so. Finally, his officer "loaned" him the cash. He got to see both of us for a few hours at the hospital. Visitors were restricted during this time to the father and grandparents. The nursery was trying to deal with an outbreak of dysentery that was taking babies' lives.

---

[20] Retrolental fibroplasia (RLF) or retinopathy of prematurity

Lady Slippers

Remember we had no penicillin[21] to treat my kidney problem or any other infections.

I must tell you about the puppy Henry had given me before we had Carol. He was a beautiful white Spitz dog. I have had dogs most of my lifetime but none that did more damage to the house than "Lucky". He didn't like to be alone. Of course, my mother and father, with whom we lived, and I, had to go to work. Lucky was confined to the kitchen and bathroom area of the apartment. Mother's sewing machine was in the kitchen. Lucky decided the electric cord was a great chew toy. He proceeded to chew it up while it was plugged in. The sewing machine was then out of order until the cord could be replaced and we moved it into the living room. Next, Lucky chewed up the linoleum on the bathroom floor, especially under the tub. The tub those days were supported by legs. To thwart him from chewing up the floor we put big tacks under there that stuck up through the linoleum. He ate them too. He even managed to mangle razor blades (still in their package) which he

---

[21] According to the University of Oxford, Penicillin became widely available in 1945. Regardless, Bernice would find out later she was allergic.

knocked off the sink. None of these sharp objects seemed to trouble him. One time we closed him in Mom and Dad's bedroom. He had a great time in there! He got under the bed and proceeded to pull all the stuffing out of the mattress. The room looked like a cotton field. It was lucky that Lucky didn't get killed that day when we came home from work.

One other great episode with him took place in another home where we confined him to the basement. When we came home, he was upstairs in the living room. We knew he couldn't open the door from the cellar. He hadn't learned that yet. The bathroom had a warm air outlet in it. The dog had gotten into the area under the bathroom through a crawl space. He knocked the metal tube that carried the warm air from the furnace to the bathroom, pushed up the heavy metal grating that covered the opening in the floor and somehow climbed through that opening. Voila! He was free to roam the entire place. And yes, he did learn to open closed doors. He would stand on his hind legs, put one front paw on the door jamb and use the other paw to hit the door knob. He would do that until he

Lady Slippers

heard the noise that told him he had turned it enough. Then he dropped to all fours and used his nose to shove the door open. He finally did himself in with all his energy and enterprise. He had a doghouse with a long chain so he could be outside. One day he got under a shed where rat poison had been placed. He ate it and died.

CHAPTER 5

Spies & Ships

1941 remains the most vivid year for me from this time period. This was the year I married my high school sweetheart. It was also the year of the attack on Pearl Harbor, Hawaii by Japan which thrust this country into a World War.

That Sunday afternoon on Staten Island, my mother and I had gone to a movie in Stapleton. Travis was a small town at the end of Victory Blvd across the Arthur Kill River from Carteret, New Jersey. Victory Blvd was a major route which spanned the island along with Richmond Terrace and Hylan Blvd. As the afternoon wore on, the film was stopped to announce to the audience what had happened in the Pacific on that day. The people were stunned as they heard of the damage and loss of lives taking place at the naval base. There was no television to show news events as they happened. We had to wait until the photographers had the pictures printed and were then sent to the newspapers which were sold on the streets. We were overwhelmed by the scope of the disaster. The men in the naval vessels had been slaughtered in their beds. Heroic efforts were made by the Air Force quartered there to get some planes up off the field and to counterattack the enemy. The losses to the United States in men and machinery were awesome.

      This attack did one thing for the United States. It united us all at once! Everyone wanted to get revenge and to strike back, so a gigantic movement started to prepare the nation for war, a war that ended up taking place on two fronts against formidable foes: the Germans, leading the forces in Europe and the Japanese, fiercely fighting in Asia. The draft of men into the armed forces targeted just about every male in the country over the age of 17-18 to 40-45. It was a major problem to train and equip that many men at one time. Everyone in the country had to sacrifice. Many factories across the nation now made items for the military from the clothes they needed to the jeeps, tanks, rifles, and ammunition. Because all the abled-bodied men were drafted into the military, the rest of the population, the elderly, and women, worked around the clock. Women became

Lady Slippers

crane operators, riveters, and did heavy laborer's work as fast as they could learn to handle the machinery. "Rosie the Riveter" became a popular song of the day, and so did overalls for women.

Other sacrifices were made on the home front. Silk stockings were not available nor coffee, sugar, butter, gas for cars, or tires. Most people who had cars put them up on blocks in the driveways for the duration. Chickens became the meat of choice with people raising their own in their backyards. They also had to learn to slaughter and pluck the birds, a very messy job. Rationing went into effect across the country. You were allowed only so much meat in a week for each person in your family. Even such things as soap and shampoo were in short supply because time could not be spent making these items but had to be spent making military things.

In our town of Travis, the new year of 1942 brought a convoy into the area. The convoy was from the Midwest and it contained an anti-aircraft unit. It lumbered up to the last street in town and moved into the abandoned linoleum factory. The buildings had been empty for a long time when the firm went bankrupt. They had no heat, electricity, or water connections at all. These men bunked on the floors of those buildings under those conditions in the middle of winter. They set up six anti-aircraft batteries to protect the skies over New Jersey. At that time, New Jersey had major petroleum refineries. Hess, Gulf and Esso[22] were prime targets. There was also Foster Wheeler, which made machine parts and American Cyanamid, a large chemical plant on the Arthur Kill. Staten Island itself was the home of Bethlehem Steel Shipyards on the North Shore on the Kill Van Kull and some other shipyard repair facilities. The Bethlehem Shipyard on Richmond Terrace had a fortified wall around it topped with barbed wire and rifle carrying guards patrolled it day and night. It was a very busy place. The island also had to protect a cable that connected all of New England to Washington with phone lines. The cable went under the Arthur Kill into New Jersey and then on to Washington D.C. Satellites in the sky didn't come until after WWII so these phone lines and radios were vital communication links.

---

[22] Esso is now owned by ExxonMobil according to Wikipedia.

Lady Slippers

In 1941, Staten Island had many piers at the entrance to New York Harbor. These piers, most of which are gone now, proved to be very valuable to the war effort. We also had a rail link across the Arthur Kill to New Jersey. Supplies came by rail into Jersey City and some came to Staten Island from all over the country. The ones that came to Staten Island ended at Tompkinsville, the far end of Victory Blvd. In the pier area, a temporary hospital was built. The ships coming back from Africa and Europe brought the wounded soldiers here, stabilized them, and then shipped them to other area hospitals. One big hospital was Halloran Hospital[23] in the Willowbrook area. This facility had been built for the handicapped children but was made ready to take the wounded servicemen. It was also used for German prisoners of war who cared for the surrounding property by cutting grass, shoveling snow and other maintenance duties. They were dressed in outfits that had PW on their backs and became a

---

[23] According to Wikipedia, after WWII Halloran Hospital became the Willowbrook State School, a state-supported institution for children with intellectual disabilities. It closed in 1987 after scandals and reported abuse. A portion of the grounds were incorporated into the campus of the College of Staten Island in the 1990s.

familiar sight to the bus passengers who passed through this facility on their way to work.

New York Harbor became a very busy place also. Because of the heavy losses to shipping in the early days of the war due to German submarine attacks, an escort convoy was set up by the United States. The Navy also mined the entrance to the harbor. The Narrows had a U-boat[24] net installed under the waterways to protect the city from attack. My father, who was 44 or 45 at the time, and had been in the army at the end of WWI, was drafted into the Coast Guard as a Chief Petty Officer. He had a pilot's license for New York City Harbor. His job was escort convoys to and from the harbor. He was called upon to lead these ships, about 50 at a time, through the Narrows, through the submarine nets and the mine fields, past the Atlantic Highlands of New Jersey, and out into the open Atlantic Ocean. There the convoy would meet the Navy destroyers who would escort the men and equipment to the battlefields in Africa, Italy, France, and Germany. It became a sight

---

[24] U-boats were German naval submarines.

Lady Slippers

we never forgot as we crossed New York's upper harbor each morning on the ferry and back again at night. The ferry had to pick its way very carefully as its path was filled with ships waiting for orders to "ship out". They seemed close enough to reach out and touch, especially in the fog that descended on the harbor at times.

The Second Armored Division, under General Patton, passed over the railroad bridge next to the Goethals Bridge and went across Staten Island to Stapleton where it was loaded onto ships on its way to famous battles in Europe.

After World War I, many of the ships that were used to ferry supplies to Europe, had been brought to protected river places. These ships had been "moth-balled". Their machinery was heavily greased to prevent it from rusting. One of these places was on Staten Island behind an island in the Arthur Kill called Prall's Island at the end of Meredith Avenue. Those ships had spent 20 years or so in that location but now found themselves towed to the shipyards to be refurbished and re-caulked. They were returned to service in the

Atlantic, carrying troops and equipment to the battlefields in Europe and Africa.

Most of us did not discuss these events in our daily lives because we were constantly warned by the radio broadcasts and reporters who told us, "Loose lips sink ships!" We obeyed because of our husbands, brothers and fathers would be the victims if those ships were lost.

Of course, we did have spies who believed in the Germans. One such person[25] lived on one of the hills overlooking the Narrows. The passage of the ships could not be covered or hidden. Therefore, anyone could see and keep track of their movements. This person watched and reported by radio any ship movements to the U-boat commander off the nearby Atlantic. The U-boats would wait for the ships to come out of the protected harbor and then track and torpedo them. They were like sitting ducks until we learned how to better protect them.

---

[25] This description matches an article titled "After 75 years, case of Staten Island Nazi spies still fascinates" on SIlive.com

Lady Slippers

One such U-boat was disabled off of Long Island during this period. It was captured and brought to a nearby dock. There it became a way for the country to help finance the war. Ordinary citizens were advised and encouraged to buy "War Bonds". These cost $18 and were held for 10 years, then could be cashed in for $25. If you had a War Bond that you bought recently, you could come to the dock, wait your turn patiently and go on tour of that captured U-boat. It was a very popular event and one which I, my young sister-in-law and my young cousin enjoyed.

New York City's LaGuardia Airport also put on a war bond effort by hosting the Airborne outfit up here. The Airborne Forces were based at Fort Bragg, North Carolina. It was a new military unit formed to drop paratroopers behind enemy lines by parachute. These forces would then be supplied by gliders with everything they would need to attack the enemy and trap them between the lines of allies. In New York City, in Dallas and other big cities, the Airborne unit put on a show so that people could see what these units could do. The show consisted of the paratroopers jumping out of the big planes and landing at LaGuardia Field. Then, three gliders at a time were loaded with small tanks, jeeps, ammunition, and food. These supplies had to be tied down in a special manner to keep them securely in place during the flight. Then they had to be able to be released with one tug upon landing. The glider was a very fragile vehicle, very light in weight and capable of flying only one way – down. It would also burst into flame if a match flared near it. A pilot and a co-pilot were in control of it. The gliders were lined up on the runway in an ordered way. Then a cargo plane would swing in low over the field, drop a rope down onto the field, snag the tow lines and fly off with all three gliders being towed behind it. The plane would then fly in a big circle over Manhattan, Staten Island, Queens, and Brooklyn, approach the field and release the tow ropes. The glider would come down onto the field, be off-loaded and the equipment would be distributed to the paratroopers. It was a spectacular sight to watch, and it earned quite a bit for the war effort. These troops were also used in Okinawa against Japan and in other areas. They suffered casualties in the 80% range. A visitor from Fayetteville offered me

Lady Slippers

her sympathies as she had witnessed first-hand many crashes during training (Henry's job). Today, Fort Bragg, in Fayetteville, North Carolina has a beautiful museum to honor the Airborne, complete with planes, gliders and parachutes.

As a tribute to the citizens at the time of the war, I must say that for the most part, people; did all that they could to help. In my own case, I remember the anti-aircraft unit who quartered right next to my house. They came to the neighbors for water daily, until the fire hydrants were opened to them. The people of Travis, upon becoming aware of conditions these men were under, gathered blankets for their use, brought out any kerosene stoves they could spare and gave them to the company. The two churches in town welcomed them to their service to provide for their spiritual well-being and companionship. Many of the citizens invited these men into their homes for meals and treated them as they would want their sons to be treated, who were also far from their own homes. Travis was a mixture of people from Europe, especially Polish people, who had come to work in the factory there and were happy to help these newcomers.

My life was changed drastically after the December 7th attack on Pearl Harbor. My husband of three months was drafted by the new year. He was chosen to be an instructor by the glider corps being formed by the army air force in Fort Bragg, North Carolina. Where I lived, the anti-aircraft unit established a gate at Victory Blvd and Wilde Ave with a sentry post. Everyone who went out of my street was stopped and asked, "Halt, who goes there?" by an armed guard.

Later on, most every person in town was fingerprinted and wore IDs with their blood type on it in case we were bombed. People became "sky watchers" and most people learned to identify our planes by their silhouettes. Since New York City was considered a prime target because of its harbor facilities and its fame, we were also under "black-out" conditions. This means that as soon as it became dusk in the evening, we had to cover our windows and doors with draperies or shutters before putting on a light. There were

Lady Slippers

patrols in the streets to make sure the rules were obeyed. Air raid sirens were on poles in various locations. If they went off, you were supposed to take shelter in your cellar. School children were told to take shelter under their desks. You were supposed to have emergency supplies to use for your family for three days. We lived under stress for the duration.

Most of the towns had outdoor plaques in a prominent spot. These signs had the names of those who were in the service from the area. Ones that had been killed had a gold star placed by their name. In addition, the homes had service flags in their windows to announce they had a person serving the country in this time of adversity. It was like a badge of honor. It was also a time of anxiety and waiting for a letter from overseas. Most of the time, you were not aware of where your serviceman was because of security reasons. You only knew if he was in the Atlantic Overseas Unit or in the Pacific Overseas Unit. This seems so different from today's news. It seems today you are actually in the same place at the same time because of the fact of television coverage and computers. It seems that the world knows everything even before the generals know of the facts or plans for our country.

The Merchant Marines were a vital part of the war effort also. They moved all the supplies and troops across both oceans. Many of these men were lost at sea. Almost all towns were devoid of men, except for the very young, very old or those with mental or physical handicaps.

At one time, the trains from the entire country from all the farms and factories ended up in Jersey City, New Jersey. There was a huge terminal there at the waterfront near the spot that now houses the Liberty Science Center and the Holland Tunnel area. The rails covered many acres of land and were filled with all kinds of equipment for the troops. The equipment was constantly being loaded onto the ships, day and night, regardless of the season or weather. A fire started in one nearly loaded ship[26]. The fire boats from New York City responded but could not put out the fire. The

---

[26] According to Wikipedia, the SS El Estero fire was started by a boiler flashback on April 24, 1943. The fireboats that responded were Fire Fighter and John J. Harvey.

ship contained ammunition of all kinds. It was decided that the ship must be towed from its location. If the fires were to reach the ammunition, it would cause a tremendous blast and would likely spread to the other equipment on the freight trains in the terminal yard. This in turn would mean the destruction of lower Manhattan and Newark in the ensuing explosion. One of the firefighters went aboard the ship and attached a tow line to it. The fire boat then towed this ship into the harbor, past the Statue of Liberty, to a spot off of Bayonne. There it was scuttled just outside the shipping lanes. It remained there until after the war ended, plainly visible to all especially at low tide. Because of the security we were under, most of the people in the rest of the country did not know of these events while they were taking place. Even people on Staten Island were not aware that anti-aircraft guns were here defending us. Most New Yorkers did not know that lower New York had almost vanished in a huge explosion except for the bravery of its fire department. These and other acts were unheralded for the most part. Everyone did more than was expected of them to reach a common goal.

As part of the war relief effort, the Red Cross had handicapped or elderly women working in various places to roll bandages by hand for the wounded. It gave out wool and instructions for making khaki-colored sweaters, mittens, socks and hats. Thus, the men were supplied with these items without the use of machines. All machine production was needed for military equipment.

CHAPTER 6

Post-War

During this time, I had stayed in my mother and father's apartment, even after Carol was born in 1943. I couldn't afford to set up an apartment on my own. We had no furniture except our bedroom set and cedar chest. The cedar chest was a gift from Henry. I did manage to fill it with sheets and towels. These were our total assets at war's end. Henry's return was a second honeymoon for us both. Carol had to adjust to a virtual stranger moving into her mother's and her own life. She had an even manner about her that helped to make the transition easier.

During Carol's early years, one of the most traumatic times was her bout with measles which turned into pneumonia. She was very ill for about three weeks. I had to keep very close care of her as the doctor didn't want her to cry. She was to be held and comforted, rocked and placated to keep her calm while she healed. She was only about ten months old at this time.

One time, when Carol was about two years old, I traveled into New York City with her. She was dressed in a knitted outfit that I made for her. It consisted of a princess style coat, leggings and bonnet, blue in color and trimmed with white angora wool. Her hair poked out in blond Shirley temple curls. We had taken a bus through Bayonne and through the tunnel into the city. The bus traveled to a terminal located down in the basement. There it went out onto a turn-table and ended up at a slot for unloading its passengers. We then went to Macy's. We ended up in the bargain basement. I was looking for materials to purchase for my mother, who would use it to make

Lady Slippers

clothes for us. I put Carol on the countertop next to me. However, the salesperson objected. She was afraid my child might fall and get hurt. I complied with her request and put Carol on the floor beside me and turned my attention back to the material. When I looked down for Carol, she was nowhere to be seen! For the next twenty minutes, a search was made for my daughter. Panic rose higher with every passing minute. The subway entrance from Macy's basement was very close. The store was crowded with shoppers. How could I go home without my child? I feared that she had been taken by a stranger. She was a beautiful little girl – a real treasure. Announcements were made over the loudspeaker alerting store personnel and everyone nearby joined in the search. At last, a peek behind the counter found my darling, calmly sitting there chewing a piece of gum! God knows where the gum came from! Did a passerby give it to her to lure her away? Or did she find it on the floor or stuck to the counter? At this point, I didn't care. I just folded her into my arms and held her so tight she couldn't breathe. I carried her back to the bus station without any further thought about shopping and boarded the bus for home. I kept her in my arms all the way home. She was totally unperturbed by all of this. She probably thought her mother was totally crazy as she had been unaware of any danger. Needless to say, my frame of mind was altogether different than hers. Hours later when my mother got home from work, she knew I was upset. I had to relive the whole episode for her. Then I had to relate the story to her father by letter. I can relate to the pain of any other mother I hear about who has lost a child even though my ordeal only lasted about twenty minutes.

My father never gave me much in the way of material things. He was a person of many talents. He knew his way around the waterfront from an early age as he signed on with a tugboat crew in Saybrook at the age of 15 or so. He quickly learned to read the ins and outs of the surrounding waterways. He contracted typhoid fever on one of these trips and was taken in unconscious and in coma to the hospital where he slowly recovered. While still in school even in the earlier days, he had managed to endear himself to his teacher. She had a horse and wagon to make her way to the one-room

Lady Slippers

schoolhouse. Her route took her past my dad's home so she volunteered to pick him up along with his sisters, Lillian and Sarah Esther (Dot), every day. In return, he was supposed to chop wood when needed and start the fire in the potbelly stove that heated the school room. One day he brought in a skunk he had trapped. He hid it during the ride to school and released it into the school room. The school had to close for three days while it was washed up and aired out – a holiday for the kids. Another time he enraged the farmer who lived next to his home by some prank or the culmination of many other pranks. Said farmer took off after him one day while he was cutting hay. He swiped my father with the scythe. The scar stayed with him for life. It went across part of his chin and down his neck just missing his Adam's apple. He was patched up with tape until he healed. He must have been a gruesome sight coming home to his mother, holding his face and neck together with his hands.

My father entered the army at the end of World War I. He was stationed on Staten Island in Tompkinsville where there was a receiving hospital. The sick and wounded were unloaded in this area, patched up a bit more, and then sent on home or to other hospitals near their families. He met my mother here. Families here and churches arranged dinners and dances for these troops. It was a chance to break up the time for both the civilians and the soldiers. You can say that I was a result of World War I.

My father then turned his talents for machinery into good use by starting up a car junk yard. When his younger brothers joined us, they benefited from his talents. They both became automobile mechanics – one in a Chevy garage in Tompkinsville and the other in a Chevy garage on Castleton Corners. They both kept those jobs all their working days. My dad was different – he was always looking for some work that was more exciting or rewarding to him. He bought a boat and turned his talents to fixing marine engines. What he liked to do best was to be given a job that could not be solved by any other mechanic. He would puzzle over it and work on it day and night until the motor worked once more. Usually, this work was for a friend, so my dad did the work for his own satisfaction and no pay for his labor.

Lady Slippers

He did get a fishing boat and took people out who wanted to fish. He could always find where the fish were hanging out on any given day. He could find his way home without visual aids in the densest fog or raging storms. One day, while fishing off the Florida coast, a sudden storm lashed the boat viciously. A lightning bolt hit the pilot house, knocking out the compass and singeing my dad. His passengers huddled in the cabin expecting to flounder any second or to be totally lost at sea, but he brought the vessel back to port. In his later years he was licensed by the Coast Guard to haul passengers anywhere on the Atlantic Coast, the St. Lawrence River, the Seaway Canal, the Great Lakes, the Mississippi River, and the Caribbean Sea. He told me that when he was 80 years old, he had just renewed his pilot's license and still was able to pass it with flying colors. This was no mean feat considering that his short formal education ended when he was able 14.

What my dad gave me that was so valuable was the gift of family. His sisters were real treasures, and his brothers could always be depended upon. Aunt Dot (Sarah Esther) was a true city person.

She sang and acted in New York City and was quite beautiful. She knew all the current dances like the Lindy and the Fox Trot and the famous Charleston. She was briefly married to a young actor, Bill. His mother was very upset. In her opinion, a young actor could not become a Matinee idol with a wife. She persuaded him to end that marriage and the child Dot was carrying immediately. He never did quite make it as a star but he did work on the stage for many years. Dot wasn't able to have children after this.

Aunt Dot then met Uncle Leo Albert. She lived with him in many places in the city. Some were fancy ones like the one above the George Washington Bridge, high above the Hudson River. One was in Washington Heights on Bennett Avenue. I was able to ride her bicycle into Fort Tyron Park up to the

Bernice and Aunt Dot

Lady Slippers

Cloisters[27] by myself. It was a very safe neighborhood then. She lived on a quiet street across from the Squibb Mansion just blocks from the park on the Hudson. She had me stay with her many times and took me out to eat in the city's many restaurants. She and Uncle Leo would give me their time and love and buy me expensive toys. She had my picture taken at my high school graduation, took me for rides in taxi cabs and added another dimension to my life. She had diamond rings and fur coats. Of course, during bad times for Uncle Leo, these things might be sold or hocked and used to pay the bills. Uncle Leo was a bookie and sometimes the odds were against him, but the bets had to be paid off. Whichever way Lady Luck favored them, up or down, their natures always seemed the same. New York City was where they chose to live, and they enjoyed the hustle and bustle of the city for many years. Leo died suddenly of a heart attack. Dot was left with no money and all their possessions were sold to give her enough money to go to Florida and live in a trailer park near her sister, Lillian. Even her dog was special – a pedigreed collie. The

---

[27] A museum specializing in medieval artwork

rest of us all had mixed breed dogs. Her dog got taken to the vet. Being feisty, Aunt Dot demanded good service wherever she went in the City. Doormen sprang to open doors for her. If the food was not to her liking, not hot or cold enough, or if a glass or utensil was dirty, there was hell to pay and everyone in the restaurant knew about the problem. She paraded around like a celebrity and her wish became her command and it was provided. No one else in either my mother's or father's family was able to get this attention that she took for granted as her right. She always had a cigarette in her hand. She was a remarkable person and a kind and caring aunt to me. It was interesting to see how children raised by the same mother and father in the same household could grow up to be so very different in their lifestyles.

    By contrast, Aunt Lillian (Lill) married Uncle Henri and raised two children through good times and bad, economically. Twice the Connecticut River flooded her family out of their home. Everything in their home that couldn't be washed and bleached had to be disposed of including pictures that couldn't be replaced.

Lady Slippers

Wherever she lived, she painted and papered it up, made it a home with tablecloths and napkins in place. Tea was always served, with a certain flair, to visitors. You felt like royalty coming to call. I spent the summer weeks with her and her children, my cousins Henri who was called Juney Bug by his mom, and Marie. I can remember biking with them down a long hill to swim in a nearby mill pond. This was an exciting place. It was on the site of an ice cutting storage yard. In the winter, the pond would freeze. Then the workers would go out onto the pond and cut the ice up into blocks. These blocks would be loaded into the building and stored covered by straw until the summer. Then they would be cut up into smaller blocks and sold to people in pieces for 25 or 50 cents. The ice man delivered these blocks to the homes and businesses in the area to be put into ice boxes. The top of the ice box had an insulated liner. The block of ice would last a day or two at a time and kept everything from going bad. You had to remember to empty the pan under the ice box every day, because the ice would melt and you'd get a flood on the kitchen floor if you forgot.

By the time we went to the mill pond, the building had been abandoned and was left empty. It was huge! There was a long once moving stairway leading to the top of the building. The blocks of ice had been placed on these steps and slowly raised to the upper reaches of storage. We romped all over this property and dove off the dock area. This called for great care. The top area of the pond was warmed by the sun. The lower depths were icy cold as the pond owed its existence to springs. The road leading to the pond was lined by fir trees. Often, we would stop our bikes and throw ourselves down on the ground that was covered by pine needles and rest. It was very pleasant to just lie there in the shade inhaling the aroma of pine and letting the sweat dry on our bodies. An air-conditioned gym could never compare with this natural way of cooling off. I benefited by being exposed to life as lived by my father's sister – a life totally different in manner from her sister in the city.

Henry was welcomed into the family by both these aunts. We spent many times with Aunt Dot and Uncle Leo in the city and many times with Aunt Lill and Uncle Henri and later with their son,

Lady Slippers

Henri and his wife, Barbara, and their children. We would stay overnight with them in Tolland, Connecticut in a home that was built in the 1700s.

Aunt Lill had her own charm as deep as Aunt Dot's but she was more focused on her children and her home. Uncle Henri, spelled with an "I" at the end because of his French ancestry, worked hard. He served in World War I and then again in World War II by laboring in an aircraft factory. He suffered from cancer at three separate times of his life, finally succumbing to it in the end. They spent a restless lifestyle of living in many different areas of Connecticut but ended their life together in a trailer park in Florida. The three older children of the Bailey family, my father, Raymond, Aunt Lillian and Aunt Dot all lived in trailer parks down there in the seventies. Aunt Dot went to a nursing home and Aunt Lill to a Senior Citizen Apartment in Tolland, until she moved in with her daughter, Marie in Ohio. She was buried with her husband, Henri in Ormond Beach, Florida while Aunt Dot is buried with her husband in Clinton, Connecticut. My dad is buried in Riviera Beach Florida with his third wife, Evelyn.

Uncle Walter, nicknamed "Buster", moved out from our home into his own. After the junk yard was sold, he got a lifetime job at a Chevy dealership. He learned from his boyhood work on cars with his brother, my father Ray. Walter had an explosive temper. I can remember when he was living with us how he'd have his sudden tantrums. Once when my flannel robe was on the stair railing, he grabbed it in his hands and ripped it apart from hem to collar! Another time he couldn't get his car to start. This is when you had to crank the car to get it to turn over. His patience exhausted, he lashed out and punched the car's radiator grill. It took a while for the knuckles on his hand to heal after being slashed open by the grill. His temper went as fast as it came. It showed up in his home life after he married Frances. You would come to visit his home and notice that they had new lamps again. If you mentioned them to Aunt Frances, she would reply good-naturedly that "Sugar" had to replace them as he had smashed them all. Thus, he earned the nickname

"Buster". I don't recall him ever hurting any people in these rages, just inanimate objects. Aunt Frances was always the life of any party. Walter was always called "Sugar" by her regardless of the circumstances. Her family had a sister Rosey who was retarded[28]. Once the parents had died, the brother took care of Rosey until he died and then Rosey came to live with Walter and Frances. Uncle Buster acquired a small boat of his own. He was a member of the Great Kills Yacht Club and a hard-working member of society. He spent the rest of his years in Staten Island. He regretted the fact that their union did not give them any children.

Hubert, my dad's other brother lived with us for many years. He learned his trade as a mechanic in the junk yard. When he was old enough, he was hired by Island Chevy on Castleton Avenue, where he labored all of his life. He also repaired many friend's and neighbor's cars free of charge whenever called upon to do so. He met Mary and they lived on Blackford Avenue where they raised three children, my cousins, George, Lillian and Irene. Mary's

---

[28] This was not a derogatory term at the time. A lot was unknown about mental disabilities.

mother, father, brothers and sisters lived upstairs. The house belonged to them.

Mary would always feed any person who dropped by to visit. This included her many brothers and sisters who'd make their way downstairs. You had to have fresh coffee or tea, a beer or shot of whiskey, and the best piece of pie or cake as she bustled about her kitchen, which was the most important room in her house. Everyone would gather around her table exchanging gossip and ideas while nibbling on something that Mary had just made on the stove or in the oven. She had many friends as she was the type of person who started a conversation with anyone she met in the stores or on the street corner. She was in walking distance of the many stores on lower Richmond Avenue, and it was her habit to browse the stores there looking for bargains. She also joined different church groups, trying out different religions at various stages of her life.

Her son (George) troubled her and Hubert, as he had a problem in school. He couldn't learn to read. Not trusting psychologists, they did not seek medical help or counseling for him.

Lady Slippers

He had difficulty finding a job. Then, when he did, he injured his back at work. He was in pain, but he, like his parents, refused to have surgery to repair damage to his spinal cord. He became a disabled person at an early age and relied on disability payments. He was married for many years, fathered two sons, and became divorced from his wife, Marge, when his children became adults. He learned to drive a car but wasn't able to hold a job.

Lillian married early in life. She and Pete raised two sons and one daughter. They were very close and spent all their time together. They traveled around the area by car and joined a folk dancing group.

Irene was the youngest child. She raised five children – three boys and two girls. Irene, Lillian, and I didn't see too much of each other when we were raising our children except on special occasions. Once our children were grown, we would see each other at least once a month, comfort each other in our losses and share our joys. My father supplied me with six aunts and uncles and five cousins, a legacy which I treasure.

My mother's family gave me another legacy of four aunts and one uncle plus their husbands, one aunt-in-law and three cousins. Aunt Emma helped us many times by taking us shopping. Bayonne had opened one of the first supermarkets in the area. It was on the border between Bayonne and Journal Square. The canned food was cheaper than A&P and Ralston grocery stores. She would buy several boxes of canned goods to make sure we had enough food to eat. Aunt Rene (Laurene) was equally helpful. Mostly they were around to take us by car on picnics and to the beach. We visited back and forth with these, our extended family.

We all gathered together at Christmas time. We spent Thanksgiving in Connecticut. We used to leave Staten Island very early in the morning and travel by ferry. Then it was a ride up the West Side of Manhattan on the overhead expressway. This took us right past all the piers that were operating their freight lines downtown. Then it was on to Fordham Road, across upper Manhattan and connecting with the Boston Post Road. This took us up through all the little towns in Connecticut where you had to be

Lady Slippers

sure you went the speed limit of 25 miles per hour. Local cops were just waiting to give you a ticket. Breakfast was in New Haven at an all night diner. Then it was onward across the Connecticut River. You would sometimes arrive with the sun, pulling into the driveway, up a hill, past the barn, and checking to see if you were the first arrival. A warm kitchen awaited you with all the good smells of the turkey roasting in the oven and the pies cooling in the pantry. Hugs were exchanged all around as were the adventures of your trip up there and a summary of your life since the last visit. Then you'd hear all that was happening in their neck of the woods. Uncle Buster and Aunt Frances and their dog, Aunt Lillian, Uncle Henri, cousins, Henri and Marie, Uncle Hubert and Mary all participated at times, though not as often as others. Aunt Mary preferred to spend the holidays with her family. Aunt Dot came most of the time. We all blended together for a family day.

    Christmas and Easter were usually spent on Staten Island meeting with other family members during visits that were paid to each other's homes for meals, gift exchanges, and just being together. It was important that no member of the family spent a holiday alone. If someone knew of another person who had no family nearby, that person was cajoled into joining us.

Before I get on with my own story, I must tell you this. People back then didn't have credit cards. If we needed something, there was Household Finance, who would lend you a small amount of money. You paid back these loans every week. There was also Mr. Richmond. He could get just about anything wholesale. He made visits by car. He sold pots and pans, coats and shoes, and even dining room sets. He would stop in once a week, collect a payment, have a cup of tea and a conversation. All the North Shore inhabitants felt his loss when he was killed by a train that collided with his car.

Here on Staten Island, we also had milk men who delivered quarts of milk to our front porch. There were insurance agents who also visited every week to supply you with life insurance for 25 cents a week. A man came around to buy any junk you had accumulated like iron, copper wire or aluminum. He had scales on his wagon or truck on which he would weigh your junk and pay you right there on the street. Another truck came around announcing his presence with a bell. His truck was outfitted with a grinding wheel. You would rush out of your home with your knives that had begun to dull. Your scissors were next, your scythe and even your ice skates also were honed and sharpened. This last service lasted until just a few years ago. The gentleman passed away and no one else has stepped up to take his place – it's the end of an era.

The day that the war ended in 1945, church bells rang from every steeple. I lit every candle in St. Anthony's Church in thanksgiving. It took me a while to pay for all those candles. As was usual, I didn't have money. I used whatever money I had and then slowly put in more money for the candles as I got it. It's a wonder I didn't burn the church down in celebration!

CHAPTER 7

Family

With the end of the war, our lives went back into the routine of work. Henry went back to the job at American Cyanamid in New Jersey. He was determined to find a better job. Therefore, he embarked on the search for something better. Every Civil service job test that came up, he took. He worked out of my mom's attic every chance he got. He also ran from Travis to Bulls Head to get himself fit enough to pass the physical exams. He also enrolled at Delahanty's in New York City. They helped him with his math, and he learned how to take Civil Service tests. He finally passed one that he wanted, for the Fire Department. The apartment upstairs in his mother's home became vacant. We had our own home at last. We partitioned a small area in the large living room and Carol had her own bedroom. We lived there for some time saving as much as we could. Our son, Paul, was born while we lived there. There was six years between Carol and Paul.

Carol was an easy child to have around. She slept easily, played contently by herself, loved to have books read to her, and sang. On buses, when we had to go shopping, she would sing, "Bell Bottom Trousers". When she started school, she learned many ditties which admonished children at the time to; remember their name and phone number, never skate on thin ice, stay away from railroad tracks and not to take their hands off their handlebars when riding their bike.

On the other hand, Paul could not be kept safely anywhere. He was ready to go and never wanted to waste a minute sleeping. For his first two years, he only slept while he was moving. A ride in the car, he slept. A ride in a carriage, he slept. Rocking in a chair, he slept. As soon as the motor or motion stopped his wails began. I learned to hang out the laundry with one hand, cook with one hand and help dress Carol with one hand. We had a walker for him. He would start at one side of the living room and get the walker moving so rapidly across the length of the room and into the bedroom which was one step lower. This resulted in a crash, which is just what he

Lady Slippers

wanted. I am talking about a baby not 10 months old. We tried putting him in a playpen. It was one that folded up for storage. He soon found out that he could move the mattress pad that covered the floor of the playpen, lift one section of the floor, get under that, and work himself under the side of the playpen and be free to investigate the entire apartment until he was captured again. From the walker he could reach the sofa back to the seat, and then to the floor. He also used the tray of the walker as a ladder into the kitchen sink where he had a great time playing with the water which he managed to get running.

While his sister tried to get ready for school, he would grab a single shoe or sock and throw it over the banister in the hallway. He learned to walk at seven months by the way. We tried to keep him happy by getting a gate for the porch, a sort of extended playpen. That only worked if you sat there and watched him. If you had a chore to do or a trip to the bathroom, he was free! He would pile up all the toys in one place and escape by climbing up them and over the gate.

Considering the fact that he never slept unless in motion, and he couldn't be confined to keep himself safe, he needed six people to keep track of him at all times. But alas, there was only me. No one else wanted to take on that task even though he was the first grandson on both sides of the family. He would catch cold easily. A simple cold would always end up as an ear infection, an infection in his throat and bronchitis. He needed his tonsils removed at a very young age.

By the time we moved to Eldridge Avenue, he settled down. He was still adventurous, but under control. One time he was outside having a conversation with our neighbor. All of a sudden, he started screaming. I ran outside but couldn't find him. The neighbor said, "He just disappeared!" We could hear him crying but couldn't see him. Finally, we figured it out. He had been sitting on the sill of the cellar window. The window had opened from the weight of Paul against it. Paul ended up on the floor of the cellar. By some miracle, the five-foot drop didn't do any permanent damage (his siblings might disagree).

Lady Slippers

It was while Paul was a baby that I really learned how to drive a car and got my driver's license. This made it much easier to go shopping. Travis only had a small grocery store. The car cut down on the time I had to spend going for food. We only had one car. Sometimes I had it and other times, Henry drove it to work.

While Carol was still a young child, my Aunt Rene suffered a terrible fall in her home. She lived alone at this time as Cousin Blair (Patrick) was married and living in his own home. Aunt Rene had walked her dog, Asta, came back into the house and locked the door. Then she reached out to hang up her coat by the cellar stairs. Somehow, she lost her balance and fell down past the landing and all the way to the cellar floor. She lay there all night unable to move. Asta lay beside her. Aunt Rene was supposed to pick up her sister, Aunt Bea, in the morning to take them both to work. When she didn't arrive, Aunt Bea started walking along the route. At first, she was angry because she knew they'd be late for work. The closer she got to the house, the more worried she became. She felt that something was very wrong. Arriving at the house, she found the door locked up tightly. She knocked several times and tried to peer into the bedroom window. By listening intently, she could hear a faint cry. She stopped a passing car. The driver was a fireman. He broke down the door and knew enough not to move Aunt Rene without help.

A trip to the hospital showed that her neck was broken at the third vertebra, as was the spinal cord. When we were allowed in to see her, we found her in a brace fastened into her skull and pulled backwards. Because the spinal cord was severed, she was paralyzed all over her body. She could only move her head and had no control over her bodily functions. She was not able to sit up in a wheelchair. Her bedroom at home became her entire world. Her family rallied around her. There were always two family members there around the clock to care for her. Dorothy, my mother, left her own home closed up for 18 months and stayed at Aunt Rene's. Then my Aunt Nan would take over and my Aunt Emma and Aunt Bea would stay for two weeks at a time. Then Aunt Marion would stay the next two weeks. Aunt Rene had to be washed at least once a day and have all

Lady Slippers

her meals fed to her. She also had to be massaged two or three times a day. It was grueling work, made worse by the fact that you knew it could only end in death. Though her arms and legs were exercised every day, her muscles atrophied. They became rigid with disuse. The one thing that saved her mind was a gadget that enabled her to read. It supported a book in an upright position, and she could turn the pages at will by using her chin. Televisions were not widely in use at this time, so reading or listening to the radio was the only entertainment available. Carol and her cousin Diane made many colored pictures for her to put up on the wall of her room. It was a dreadful thing to see a vibrant being reduced to an immobile body. It bothered her very much emotionally because she was aware of the stress and strain, she was imposing on her family. A moment's inattention and disaster struck her. She had almost reached her personal goal of becoming the boss in charge of her office as her boss had been planning to retire. She was next in line to take over, a big career leap for a woman in those days. That dream ended in pieces with the fall. She had built a good life for herself and her son

Blair. Blair's father had abandoned them when Blair was about 10 months old. He just walked out. Rene had gotten her high school diploma by going to night classes at Curtis High School. This meant a long walk to Bulls Head and traveling to Port Richmond by trolley car, transferring to the trolley on Richmond Terrace and then a hike up a hill from St. George to Curtis to classes. This was after working all day. She managed to raise her son, buy a home and a car, all on her own. She was also determined that her younger sister, Marion would finish high school, and then continue in school to become a registered nurse. She had me come in to clean her house on Saturdays when I was a teenager so I would have some "spending money". She was a loving, giving person. She took my mother, cousin, and me to visit other cousins, Bennetts, who lived in Highland Park, New Jersey. Her fall finally claimed her life. After she died, we lost track of these other relatives.

    Returning to my immediate family, once Paul got mobile, he became easier to manage. We moved to our current residence on Eldridge Avenue when he was three. We were still living in crowded

Lady Slippers

conditions as our house was a two family. That meant we had a sunporch, a small living room and a bedroom, that should have been a dining room. We used the sunporch as a bedroom for Paul. Carol slept on a folding bed in an alcove off the kitchen. This enabled us to use the rent from the upstairs apartment to double the mortgage payments each month.

In order to pay the mortgage off even quicker, Henry did roofing jobs on his days off from the fire department. He also did room painting and put up wallpaper. With all of these extra jobs, we still found time to take trips to Asbury Park, New Jersey. Our friend Jessie from Travis always rented a place in Asbury Park for the summer months. We would meet her on the beach, use her pool club bathhouse to change into swimwear and have a great day in the water. Then we would again use the pool club facilities to have a hot shower and dress in street clothes. We would then have dinner out. Sometimes we even rode on the merry-go-round, a centuries old one with hand-carved horses. We ended up with a one day vacation marvel except for the sunburns that we usually got.

One day we did get to take a sightseeing trip to Maine. We wanted to see the sand dunes, but the day we were there was the day they were closed. We drove up to Lake Winnipesauke. It was a beautiful lake with a deserted beach front. So we stopped and I decided to take a quick swim. It was a really quick swim! I dove into the water with a running start, turned around and raced out of the water as if a school of sharks was chasing me! That was the coldest water I have ever felt. I was purple and could barely get back into clothes fast enough. Talk about ice water. I still shiver just thinking about it.

We traveled by excursion boat up the Hudson River and debarked at Bear Mountain. There we could hike to the top of Bear Mountain overlooking the Hudson River, swim in a pool, walk around the lake or go rowing out on it and have a picnic. They did have bears there confined to cages.

We also went to Palisades Park which also had a pool and many rides to keep us busy for the day. I remember that Paul got on the small Ferris wheel, one for little children. He decided he didn't

Lady Slippers

like going up and started yelling so the ride attendant brought him down and let him off. Every other rider wanted off immediately also. The attendant was pretty busy trying to placate 6 or 7 crying kids and give them back their tickets. There was a nice picnic area there near the parking lot under some trees. It was a great place but they tore it down to make way for housing, so our younger two didn't get to enjoy the place at all.

My mother and father got divorced after 25 years of marriage. At this point, my father moved to Florida to live. He was in Riviera Beach, where he took out fishing parties. They took out three parties each day. As mentioned before, on one occasion his boat was struck by lightning. The bolt wiped out all of the marine equipment and singed his arms and face. His passengers figured they were all about to be "lost" at sea. However, he was able to bring the boat back to the dock by "dead reckoning". It had been a scary outing for all of them.

I lost touch with him for a long time after that. I felt he had hurt my mother so much during their marriage. He was a womanizer, having many women "friends". He married one of them after the divorce but that didn't last too long. He didn't get to know any of his grandchildren at all. He should have been here to share some of his talent with them. He had a lot of stories of his varied life, but all of these were lost to his grandchildren. These are some of the reasons I did not contact him much after he moved. I think he stopped here one time when Paul was about two years old.

Just about the time Paul turned six, we had our third child, a son we named Steven. He was a calm baby, more like his sister, Carol than his brother, Paul. We had taken over the whole house by this time, so now we had three bedrooms upstairs and a full bathroom. The living room was much bigger too because the hallways that led from the front door to the staircase had been removed. We also had a dining room for the very first time and a closet in each bedroom. Being able to have this much space was marvelous. Carol had her own private room and Paul and Steven shared a bedroom.

Lady Slippers

During all of these years, Fourth of July was a special occasion. Travis has an old fashioned hometown parade. We'd always get our favorite spot on Cannon Ave where there is a place to put our chairs in the shade. Travis has one of the only two volunteer fire departments in New York City. They have contacts with all the volunteer companies in New Jersey, so they all come to march in the parade. The watchers bring water guns or horses out and they have water fights with the fire trucks. Usually, it is a blistering hot day so the water refreshes everyone, watchers and marchers alike. There are a lot of bands and old vintage cars. After the parade, most families have all day picnics. Whole families get together to hang out all day long. The houses in Travis are decorated in patriotic motifs and American flags line the streets. You must be off Victory Blvd by 11AM as the police stop traffic through the town at that time. The politicians come out in force, stopping by to shake hands with the people lining the streets. Everyone gets involved. People who used to live in Travis come back, walk along Victory Blvd to P.S. 26 and greet their neighbors. Clowns come up to children and exchange hugs with them while their parents take pictures. It is a really nice day for all. There are no fences or barriers along the parade route to separate marchers from the watchers.

Travis is also changing now as the island grows. So many new homes have been built in every available space that it is not a small town anymore. The newcomers do not have any long-time ties to the area, and it is too early to know if they will adopt the old traditions and improve on them or if they will want to do away with the old ways of celebrating the 4th.

Since we moved to Eldridge Avenue, my three children now attended Blessed Sacrament School[29]. The school ran a fair every year. The Mother's Club organized it as a way to raise money to use for the school. It started as a "Penny Sale". This was fine for a while because things were cheaper and expenses for the school were cheaper too. Most of the teachers were nuns. Times changed and fewer nuns were available to teach. Lay teachers had to be paid a salary and health benefits. Other expenses also went up. The fair had

---

[29] A private Christian school near the Westerleigh area, serving grades Pre-K through 8th. Reference: https://blessedsacramentsi.com/

included crafts that were fashioned by the mothers, like knitted outfits, Afghans, toys, doll clothes, aprons, and hand-made ornaments. Prices went up and so did the money raised by this two day event. Mothers gathered up all the toys and books that their children grew tired of and abandoned. These were donated to the used toy and book part of the fair. It was frustrating when your children gleefully bought one of these great bargain toys because he had one at home just like it! Mothers worked from Christmas to Christmas getting ready for this event. One of the best features was the luncheon on Sundays. It had two seatings and was always a surprise meal for the participants. Each mother brought in a dish that she usually made at home for the family like baked macaroni and cheese, lasagna, fried chicken, baked beans, or ravioli. The list was varied. Salads were in abundance and there were a variety of desserts as well.

    The children at this fair were able to play games and win prizes, have their face painted in various patterns, pay a visit to Santa Claus and get out of class on Friday. They went shopping for treasure for their moms, dads, and grandparents to use as Christmas presents. A lot of the items at the fair were donated by local merchants, like dinners for two at a restaurant. To receive these gifts, people would have to make many "begging" visits to all the area businesses to convince them that this was a good advertising ploy. After working on the fair for many years myself, I knew how much time and work went into every fair. The people who gave their time and talents should be recognized for their efforts. It is the reason that the school had been able to buy the goods and services it needed to keep the school up to par with costs that tuition didn't cover.

Just about the time that Carol graduated from high school, we had David, our fourth child. I had had a spontaneous miscarriage when Steven was about three. It left me a bit depressed as we had been looking forward to becoming parents again. Also, I was getting older and doctors didn't approve of having babies after the age of forty (because of higher risk to the mother and child). The birth was a real hard one. The baby was supposed to arrive in July like Paul and Carol but he chose June 9th instead. He started three days before that but once labor started, he stayed inside. He was presenting chin first. My doctor tried to reach in and change his position because he was in danger of breaking his neck. But he would not be moved. She, my doctor, called in a colleague to assist her. She had already told Henry to expect the worst. In her experience, most of these births resulted in death or at the very least a broken clavicle. When they finally peeled David out of me, he didn't cry immediately, and she didn't show him to me. I sat up and broke the restraints on my arms to try and see my baby. The doctor said, "He seems okay, relax. He doesn't look very good as he has a black eye and his face went through quite an ordeal." He was just about 5 pounds and 17 inches long. It was a real problem to find any clothes that fit him. Even the smallest undershirts were way too big. Fortunately, he gained weight. However, for many months, when you lay him down in his crib, he turned his head backwards. Because of his difficult birth, we chose Jude as his second name since Jude was supposed to be the saint of Impossible Causes.

This child was a tantrum child. When he was told "No!" he would throw himself on the floor and drum his heels and scream. I learned early on that the only way to stop the tantrum was to isolate him in a room until he controlled himself. As he grew older, he would go up to his own bedroom, rant and rave saying, "Nobody loves me!" and then come back down when he calmed down. One day he threw his fit in his closed closet. When he was ready to come out, the door stuck, and he had a heck of a time getting out. The tantrums seemed to stop after that.

Having three boys in the house caused other problems. They shared one bedroom with one closet. At first, Paul and Steven shared a bed. However, I soon realized it wasn't working. I would go into the room to check on them and find Paul wrapped up in all the bedclothes and Steven huddled with no sheets or covers on him at all. I put them both in single beds and then Steve at least got to keep his covers. We had a youth bed for Dave. So now we had three beds in that room. It was a good thing that computers weren't in wide use

Lady Slippers

then as there wasn't any room for one. No one had TVs in their rooms then either.

Paul was fascinated with trains as a child. Whenever you went riding on car trips, he'd get all excited seeing a passing train. "I want to see another train," he would repeat over and over. We had the Arlington train yards in Mainers Harbor. The trains would come in from New Jersey over the railroad bridge that paralleled the Goethals Bridge. They would then be shuttled onto side tracks and reassembled into freight cars ready for their new destinations. Paul loved to be taken to that spot and watch whatever activity was going on at the time.

We bought him a train table for the cellar. Over time it became a two-line train set with mountains built from scratch and bridges over a river. It had an airfield, a shopping center, gas station, and a spot where the two lines would meet and cross. As he became older, he would program the trains to meet at that crossing and we would have a messy train wreck. Other neighborhood kids would come in to play with the trains and hang out especially on days when the weather outside was bad. I had to make a rule that each kid could only have one friend at a time over to play. Otherwise, it quickly got out of hand. I also had to put a limit on how many sodas each one could have, or the house would be cleaned out of snacks in an hour by six boys!

Sometimes I would take all the boys crabbing in Tottenville near the old Perth Amboy Ferry. There were old barges there that had been abandoned by the owners and run aground. Over the years, many fires had been started on these barges. It was an adventure to balance oneself high on the barge about 15 feet from the water, carrying bait, crab-pots, lunches, and drinks, across charred beams out to the river front. At low tide the front of the barge was out of water, but as the tide came back in, the planks would be covered with water. Also, every passing vessel would make waves that encroached up onto the barge. Planks, when wet, became slippery with slime and moss. You had to have a deep basket to empty crabs into. We managed to not fall overboard and to not fall into the interior of the barge. We did come close to disaster one time when

Lady Slippers

Tommy, a neighbor's boy's leg went through a plank. Fortunately, he didn't break any bones, but he did get scratched up. We had to wash his leg down with our drinking water to clean the wound. We bandaged it using the first aid kit in my car.

We also took our dog along. He loved to be with the other kids and he loved to go to the waterfront with us. He could walk those beams pretty well and drank whatever we had – iced tea, soda or water. The only problem with catching crabs is they had to be cooked as soon as you got home. We all enjoyed eating them though.

Our lives were busy with all the children and their activities filled much of the time in those years. Carol developed allergies in her teen years. We had to find a doctor who would treat her. The treatment consisted of a series of shots every week. It was quite scary when she had an attack of asthma because every breath came labored. I remember one time when she went on a date with her friend, Stuart. They went on a hayride. By the time he brought her home, she was wheezing so loudly I could hear her outside in the car. The date was more than eager to get her into the house and leave. He was afraid she was going to pass out and he didn't want to have to deal with that problem. Many nights I slept on the floor in her room with a vaporizer on all night. She would be fine for a while and then suddenly encounter one or more allergen and be overcome with breathing difficulties.

Paul never had a <u>simple</u> cold until he finally outgrew his tendency to have strep throats. He also used to hallucinate and walk in his sleep whenever he had a high fever. Steve had no major problems. His allergies waited to plaque him in adulthood. Dave had some problems as his colds tended to turn into bronchitis.

Lady Slippers

CHAPTER 8

The Accident

Paul, Bernice, and Steven visiting David in the hospital.

When Dave was just under five years old, we were in a major car accident. My mother, David, and I had been shopping for our weekly groceries. It was a rainy afternoon, so we decided to drive to Port Richmond High School and pick up Paul. As we came down Jewett Ave, a gas company truck came out of College Avenue, struck our car on the left rear side and pushed it into a telephone pole near the corner. My mother was driving, I was in the front passenger seat, and Dave was standing on the floor in the back of the two-door

131

car. Cars were not equipped with seat belts then (1964)[30]. I was thrown out of the car into the gutter onto Jewett Ave. My mother was thrown out of the car from behind the wheel and past where I had been sitting and landed on the grass between the sidewalk and the curb.

All the groceries ended up hitting Dave who was still in the back seat. He was screaming in the car and my mom was lying on the ground. I was trying to get back to Dave as I was afraid the car would go on fire as the motor was still running. My pocketbook had fallen out with me. Paper money was floating down the gutter. I grabbed it, or as much as I could while trying to get back into the car. Now it seems like such a "dumb thing" to have been worried about at the time. I was able to turn off the motor and drag Dave from the backseat and hold him in my arms. Neighborhood people called the police and the fire department. Someone covered my mom with a blanket and another person held an umbrella over her head. I thought she had died because she lay there unmoving all this time.

---

[30] Federal Law began mandating all new cars be equipped with seats belts in 1968. Reference: www.cdc.gov

Lady Slippers

Dave's face and wrists were bleeding. The windows hadn't broken into sharp pieces of glass but the smaller fragments took out little pieces of his skin wherever they hit him. His one leg seemed swollen and spongy so I thought it may be broken. I tried to clean some of the blood from him to make sure he wasn't hemorrhaging but the cuts did not seem too threatening. The fire department arrived before the ambulance.

All of us were bundled up into the ambulance and we made a quick trip to the emergency room. There I had to give permission for them to operate on David if that was necessary. They cut his clothes off and put me out of the room. All I could do was sit by myself and wait to hear the doctor's decision. By the end of that day, I learned that my mother had a concussion and a cut on her forehead, but nothing else showed up. Dave had a broken femur. In growing children, they treat these fractures by putting both legs in traction, so they remain the same length during the healing process. The legs got wrapped up and ten-pound weighs were fastened on the ends to keep the bones aligned for a six-week period.

This was a very exhausting time for us all. I had gone home which was a mistake. I had three days when I was literally in shock. Driving home, I was afraid of every car that came near ours. I couldn't lie down and sleep – I was shaking so much. Carol held me and tried to get me to relax. I insisted upon going to the hospital twice a day to see both parties. Dave did not want me to leave him. All the way down in the elevator we could hear him screaming. Hospital practice at this time would not permit parents to stay with their children except during visiting hours.

We didn't know anything about the surgeon who was treating David, so we had a specialist check him out and get a second opinion. We were told it was a bad break with many vertical cracks on both sides. After reviewing the procedures, our specialist concurred with the surgeon's recommendations. There were three other boys in the room with Dave and two others were in traction like he was. One other 2 ½ year old boy from a room farther down the hall had had open heart surgery done on him. He was recovering nicely. Staff was trying to keep him confined to his crib when his

Lady Slippers

parents weren't there with him. There was a top over his crib, but he found a way to get out and climb down to the floor. He'd take off down the halls. He'd come into David's room and gleefully start swinging the weighs on Matthew's Richard's and David's legs. All three boys would yell and push their call buttons until finally a nurse would hear the commotion and return the heart patient to captivity.

David had problems with the weights. He only weighed 25 pounds himself, so the weights were heavy enough to pull him to the bottom of the bed. The staff had to attach a harness of sorts to his upper body and fasten that to the top of the bed to keep him in place. Another problem with traction patients is that they have to wear diapers. They cannot use bedpans. Dave didn't want anyone to visit him and see him in diapers as it was too embarrassing for him. We solved that problem by opening up the side seams of his shorts and added zippers to them. Now the diapers were hidden from sight. In addition, the harness which attached him to the top of the bed prevented him from eating his meals by himself. He began losing weight. One of the nurses brought in bread and peanut butter and made him sandwiches as a snack. We also started bringing him food twice a day and fed it to him. David did nothing to relieve my mother's guilt over the accident. As soon as she was able to visit him, he asked her why she let that truck hit us.

About four days after the accident, I had to go to the doctor myself. I had injured my leg when I was thrown from the car and because I was so concerned about Mom and David, I didn't realize how badly I had been hurt. I was going to the hospital twice a day and walking on it – the injury was getting worse and worse. It was diagnosed as a hematoma[31] all along my shin bone. It had to be treated with water therapy, pain killers, and rest.

After six weeks in traction, David was allowed to come home. However, he was not allowed to put any weight on that femur at all. He got around the house by himself by scooting around on his butt. I still had trouble riding in a car unless I was driving the car myself. David was home about one week or so when he hitched himself up the stairs to the second floor. He had almost reached the

---

[31] A solid swelling of clotted blood within the tissues.

Lady Slippers

top when Steven greeted him with a "BOO!" This startled Dave who lost his precarious perch on the step and tumbled end over end all the way down the stairs. Paul heard the commotion and ran down the sidewalk yelling for Dad to come back home and telling him why. Steve, not believing what his action had caused, retreated into his room. I guess he thought he was going to get killed. I couldn't believe it myself. I rushed to Dave and grabbed him up in my arms and put him in the bathtub, clothes, and all. I was crying and couldn't bring myself to even think of David back in the hospital for another six weeks. Henry raced home and between us we came to the conclusion that he suffered no ill effects from the fall except for a bruise or two. After all that tension, Steven even dared to come out.

  Finally, the day came when the doctor allowed David to walk again. He actually had to learn how to do it as if for the first time. He tended not to lead out with the injured leg. He led with the other and brought the injured leg up to join the first leg. We got him help by taking him to the "Y" and into the water. Our friends belonged to the YMCA and they took us in 5 or 6 times. By the end of summer, his leg had healed. But emotionally, he suffered from the same fears that I had. Twice he thought that we were going to be hit by another vehicle. He opened the door of the car both times and tried to get away. This was very dangerous since the car was still moving. We had to watch him carefully until his mind learned to cope. My mom also had residual fears and at times almost drove up on the right-hand side curb (since she had been hit on the left). We all avoided the intersection where we were struck for a very long time.

Lady Slippers

CHAPTER 9

College & Thugs

Bernice, David, and Dorothy (Mom) with dogs, Jacques and Patsy at Wolfe Pond Park in Staten Island.

All of the years that my family was growing up, I suffered from migraine headaches. They were very bad. I couldn't stand any noise and the smell of food cooking was enough to send me into the bathroom for hours. I was sent to New York City where they treated only headaches but to no avail. The doctors started me on pain shots.

The shots worked but I had to have someone drive me home as I would fall asleep on the way. The shots didn't prevent the headaches from coming again over and over. Finally, the shots were discontinued so that I wouldn't get hooked on the drugs. I guess this ailment runs in families. My mother told me of all the times her mother had to go to bed for three days in a darkened room with a cold cloth over her eyes. My mother had the same ailment and so did her sisters. I remember sitting on the floor and hitting my head on the wall. Of course, that didn't make it pleasant to be around me during these attacks. They lasted for years.

In spite of all the problems that came along with everyday life, we managed to get four kids through grade school, high school, and college. Each problem was faced and conquered. The boys all had part time jobs during college. Steven and David had thugs, who tried to rob them, come into the businesses where they were working. The thugs had guns. The one time the police took David around to nearby bars looking for the thief. I didn't like that at all. This guy had a gun and he could have used it on Dave to get rid of

Lady Slippers

an eye witness especially if he had felt threatened. Dave also had a bad accident. He was preparing chicken for frying at KFC and he slipped on something on the floor. He fell into the slicing machine. Two fingers on his right hand were sliced open. One had a ligament severed. He couldn't write for a long time after that. He did learn to bowl with his left hand and did pretty well.

Steven got hurt on the job also. He hurt his hand working in a paint store. The back of his hand had a large piece gouged out of it by a shelf. It took a long time to heal as the skin had to fill back in.

Meanwhile Carol had graduated from Notre Dame College, spent a year at the University of Wisconsin in graduate school and was a third grade teacher at P.S. 23. Carol went on a trip to Bermuda to visit her friend Myra. She introduced Carol to George at the base beach. Myra was checking in the swimmer's baskets of clothes and George was a lifeguard. They had been corresponding for several months and George came home in February of 1968 and proposed. George was between assignments – his next base would be Ellsworth in South Dakota. He was staying in New York to meet us and to travel to Pennsylvania to meet his family and make wedding plans. He was from the town of Lebanon in Pennsylvania Dutch country and a fireman in the US Air Force.

One evening they went into the city to see the play, *Mame*. It was too late to catch the last ferry to Staten Island, so they were in the Port Authority Bus Station waiting for a bus to bring them back to Staten Island. They were sitting at a coffee counter having something to eat. Carol had her purse on the floor between her feet and suddenly discovered that it had been stolen. They reported it to the Port Authority Police who told them it was the 5th one that day. When they got home, they told us what happened. There was very little money in the wallet but some Carol's teaching papers for school, her driver's license, checkbook, social security number, and keys to her car and the house were in her purse. The next morning, Henry decided to go into the city. He reasoned that a thief would take the cash and other valuables and ditch the pocketbook itself as soon as possible. He rode up there and started searching all the trash

Lady Slippers

cans in the vicinity. He asked people if they had seen anything and offered a reward for the return of the contents of the purse.

About 11AM that next day, I got a phone call asking me to come to the Port Authority to meet with "John" who would be standing on the corner outside because he had found Carol's purse. I checked with a policeman friend who told me to call the Port Authority Police Station. They told me to make sure my house wasn't empty. Sometimes, a resident is lured out of the house and then an accomplice comes in and robs it. I was instructed to go directly to the Police Station when I got to the Port Authority Building. When I got there, they told me to go to the corner that "John" had suggested and ask him, "Are you John?" They planned to follow me and observe with men in plain clothes. I felt like I had a part in a movie as I walked through that big busy bus terminal. It was unreal. My heart was thumping as I reached the street and turned left. I was positive that I was alone. A man was waiting there. I asked if he was John. When he said, "Yes" from out of nowhere four cops had him. I could breathe again.

It turned out that John was not an innocent bystander who "found" Carol's bag. When they checked his room, they found that he had been practicing her signature and had tried to cash one of her checks. He was wanted by the police in New Jersey. The most important thing was that all of her papers were returned to her. It was an interesting adventure for George but only reinforced his big city anxieties.

Because George was in the Air Force, he was subject to frequent moves and of course, Carol for the most part was able to accompany him. This gave us the opportunity to join them in new places and experience many adventures with them. After their marriage in 1968, Carol and George lived in Rapid City, South Dakota where he was stationed at Ellsworth Air Force Base. He was a firefighter and then became trained in fire extinguisher and alarm systems. Their first child was Laurie Ann.

Lady Slippers

CHAPTER 10

Laurie

Bernice, George, and Kris on the Staten Island Ferry.

My mother and I shared a plane trip (my mother's first airplane ride ever) to Rapid City to visit her great granddaughter. Laurie was a very special child and the only great granddaughter my mom ever got to see. The arrival was an experience in itself as the airport there felt like we were landing in a cow pasture. It was a wonder a large plane could land there at all. While in South Dakota, we visited the Badlands. It was December so we were the only visitors. In fact, I think we were the only ones alive out there. We parked in the one area and got out to look at the fossils. They were encased in glass containers to protect them from the weather and the people who'd take "samples" home with them. You can't drive off the road there as the dirt is a clay mixture. Once it became wet, it becomes impassible and it is very slippery, like being on ice. This is one place you really needed a cell phone (if you could get service). All you hear out there is the weird sound of the wind as it passes over the area. It made me laugh because my Mom automatically locked the car doors.

We stopped at a place called Wall Drug[32] – a famous tourist trap. All along the highway there were signs which give the distance to Wall Drug. These signs are posted all around the world – we did spot one years later in Amsterdam. There were all kinds of souvenirs there that you could buy including a "Jackalope". Wall Drug

---

[32] A small-town drug store that grew into a cowboy themed mall and department store thanks to its advertising efforts and location near Mt. Rushmore, according to Wikipedia.

Lady Slippers

reminded me of the South of the Border[33] store on the way to Florida along Rte. 95. The town of Wall consisted of a single street.

We also went to see Mount Rushmore. I had seen pictures of the president's heads carved out of the mountainside, but nothing prepares you for its huge size. All the dimensions are listed such as the length of Washington's nose, but when you actually see it, it doesn't register. The four famous faces are Washington, Jefferson, Lincoln, and Teddy Roosevelt. I think they are as surprised to find themselves up there, as we are to see them there. Washington's head is taller than a five-story building (60 feet). Workers actually hung on ropes suspended over the cliff and blasted these images into being. It was magnificent.

To reach the "faces", we had to travel through Custer State Park. Rangers warn you to stay inside your car. Those buffalos are mighty big, and they often charge the cars. The jackasses that roam free inside the park are ones that escaped from the wagon trains that passed this way on their way to California. They have become wild

---

[33] Located in Hamer, South Carolina, just south of Rowland, North Carolina.

and you are warned not to feed them. But of course, they will stick their heads right inside your car windows begging for treats. There are no gates in the roadways of the park. Instead, there are open grates across the pavement that the animals will not cross as their legs slip through the slats. The buffalo are protected from hunters and are making a comeback as to numbers, but they are nowhere near the vast numbers that used to roam the prairies. Some ranchers are raising them for food. Even here in New York you can buy a buffalo burger in some restaurants.

When we went home, we had to stop in the twin cities of St. Paul and Minneapolis to transfer to a bigger plane. We were racing down the runway which had to be plowed to give us a passageway. Suddenly the pilot slammed on the brakes. Everyone held their breath waiting for the ensuing crash! The pilot came on the intercom, apologized for the abruptness of the stop and the scare, and explained that a small plane had landed unexpectedly on the runway and cut right in front of him. We missed a crash by inches – what a close call!

Lady Slippers

After only about two years of marriage George was assigned a remote tour to Suwon, Korea (it could have been Vietnam). Families were not permitted to travel there as living conditions were sub-standard. So, Carol moved into Aunt Emma's house on Staten Island for this time with Laurie and their cat, Ling. Carol and Laurie spent a lot of time with us during that year. The boys felt as if they had a baby sister and she was a fun toddler to be around.

One day especially remains in my mind of Laurie before her illness. While she was here on Staten Island, she and Carol attended mass at Blessed Sacrament Church. This was an Easter Sunday. We had been seated in the center of the church near the center aisle. Carol and Laurie came in later and were taking seats near the front of the church. Laurie spotted me and came running toward me calling as she did so, "Nanny, Nanny!" The picture of her happy smiling face remains stored forever in my mind.

After George's return, he was assigned to Castle Air Force Base in California. They drove across country and were still living in a motel as base housing wasn't available and they hadn't found a place to rent. They noticed something wrong with Laurie's eye. It shined like a cat's eye at night. Laurie was sent to an ophthalmologist in town and then to Travis AFB and finally to the Presidio in San Francisco. The diagnosis was bilateral retinoblastoma – a cancer of the retina. It usually occurs in children under the age of five years old and is caused (we found out much later) by a double mutation. Sometimes it can run in families, but we had no knowledge of that. Laurie had to have her eye removed. Radiation and chemotherapy were tried to save her other eye and her life, but the cancer had spread to her whole body.

When Carol knew Laurie would become blind, she started teaching her Braille. She taught Laurie how to dress herself by setting out outfits that matched in piles. Laurie had gotten sick in September when she was almost three. During this time, Laurie coped with her tragedy in her own special way. She was very conscious of the fact that her hair had all fallen out due to her treatment. She would not leave the house without putting on her hat. She didn't want anyone to see her bald head.

Lady Slippers

After both eyes had been removed to stem the spread of the cancer, she wore both hat and sunglasses outside. Once at the doctor's office, another child commented to her parents that that kid looked silly wearing her sunglasses inside. Laurie faced the commentator, removed her sunglasses, exposing her empty eye sockets and calmly said, "Now you can see why I keep hat and glasses on even inside" Adults and children alike were shocked by her appearance and embarrassed as well.

Laurie suffered terribly until she was almost four. During this time, David and I traveled to California to be with Carol and George. We spent time in San Francisco at the Presidio (Letterman Military Hospital). I would try to take David out in between visits to Laurie whose last hospital stay was up there. We did get to ride the trolley down hills, walked around Fisherman's Wharf and one day we took a trip by tour bus to Muir Woods to see the giant redwoods. David was only twelve at that time. It was a tough time for him. When you went into the hospital, you not only saw your little relative, but you noticed all the other suffering little kids. It can't help your own mental state to see how much distress was in those hospital rooms.

We were with them when they brought Laurie home to Merced. The final dose of chemotherapy was not helping. A month before that, Carol and George's second daughter, Kristen Marie was born. She was the only bright spot that year (1973), though it was hard to care for a newborn and have another child critically ill at the same time. Because we were doing all this traveling with a newborn, Kris, we had her baptized at the Presidio without any proper outfit to wear or any other celebrations, just the knowledge that she was a child of God. Laurie received the sacrament of Confirmation once she was home in Merced. She couldn't have Communion because she was unable to swallow at that time. A short time later she went into a coma and finally found peace.

CHAPTER 11

1973

My mother also traveled to Merced with me at one point – we arrived via San Francisco. We got to explore Merced many times over the years, visiting Yosemite National Park, panning for gold in the Merced River and looking at the ugly turkey vultures perched in the trees. We visited Monterey, saw Pebble Beach Golf Course, crossed over the Golden Gate Bridge, saw San Quentin Prison and visited Sacramento's train museum. We also saw a working seismograph machine in San Francisco, which was continually registering some amounts of earth movement. We rode the trolley up and down hills and spent time at Fisherman's Wharf. Along the one highway, you could plainly see the fault line with one side being higher than the other and slanted sideways. We even saw real live scorpions and tarantulas up in the foothills. We made sure we didn't meet up with any snakes as we made lots of noise so they would leave.

1973 was a terrible year for me – I lost 5 family members that year. My Uncle Roy, husband of Aunt Bea, died first. Next, my mother and I had gone to New York City on a Sunday to be with my Aunt Dot. Her husband, Uncle Leo had had a heart attack and died the day before. We spent the day with Aunt Dot cooking a meal for her and coaxing her to eat a little and to have a cup of coffee. We tried to comfort her as best we could. They had been together a long time and Uncle Leo had not been sick, so it was quite a shock. Mom and I left Aunt Dot promising that we would be back the next day to help and do what needed to be done there. We got into Mom's car at the ferry parking lot and I started driving to my house. As we drove along Richmond Terrace, we were admiring the beautiful sunset that you sometimes see on a cold clear day in January. The sun was just dropping behind the Bayonne Bridge and the sky was still a beautiful rosy color.

 Mom suddenly said, "Bernice, pull over to the curb!" She seldom called me Bernice. It was either Bern or Hon. This was a sharp command! I started to slow the car and pulled to the side of the

Lady Slippers

road when she slumped forward. Thank God that she had her seatbelt on as it prevented her from continuing her slump to the floor. I tried to get her to respond to me as I drove the car as fast as possible to the hospital. I went the wrong way on a one-way street hoping a policeman would interrupt me and I even went through a red light. Reaching the Emergency Room, I raced inside shouting for help. The response was rapid and efficient. I paced the floor but, in a few minutes, they came to tell me that she was gone.

I had to call her brother, Bob, and notify him but I couldn't remember his phone number. The people in the Emergency Room looked it up for me and reached him at home. He and Aunt Nan made the trip to the hospital. I couldn't drive the car and had to call my brother-in-law to get my son, Paul to come for me. Henry had left for work at the firehouse, so he was not available.

Later that evening, Aunt Dot's brother, Uncle Hubert called. I was supposed to have called them on Sunday when I got home to tell them about Uncle Leo's funeral plans. They were astonished when I told them about my mother. We now had two funerals to go through at the same time. Even my father heard the news in Florida and called to ask, "What happened to your mother?" It was a really rough time for all of us.

As we look back on it now from a distance, we can all say of Mom's passing, "That's the way to go." There was no suffering for years like cancer patients endured. All of her faculties were intact. She was not alone at home. She had medical help within minutes. A little bit later on that day she would have been driving herself home alone or would have arrived at her house and been by herself. After she had seen how her sister, Laurene had died because of her fall and subsequent paralysis, Mom's wish had been to have a peaceful death with no nursing home incarceration and no long hospital stay.

It is amazing how much the human spirit can stand of loss and panic. What gives us the courage and will to go on? I had driven the car many blocks to the hospital that day but couldn't drive it any further after the loss of my mother. After Laurie passed away, she was brought back here to Staten Island to be buried with her great-grandmother. My mom knew that Laurie's illness was terminal and

Lady Slippers

had requested that she be brought here to the family plot. Little did she know that she would die before her great-grandchild.

The same day that Laurie was buried here on Staten Island, my Uncle Henri, Lillian's husband would be buried in Florida. I obviously couldn't attend both funerals.

Our second granddaughter, Kris had a very different personality than Laurie. Laurie seemed to love everyone around her. Kris seemed to be self-contained. People were okay but she was sufficient by herself. She didn't want to be called pet names and would inform you in no uncertain terms that her name was not anything else but Kris. When she was 2 ½, she fell from a jungle gym in a park onto a dirt surface. She was very ill the next day with a high fever and complained of aches and pains. She was put on baby aspirin (treatment at the time), but the fever did not go away. She wasn't eating or drinking and had a rash which the first doctor brushed off as "measles" – although she had had all of her shots and should have had a milder case. Carol asked for another doctor, and he hospitalized her at Castle Hospital for dehydration. While on fluids, she developed a lump over her collarbone. Kris was referred to the head of the children's oncology department at the Presidio. Of course, after having lost Laurie to cancer three years earlier, we were all frantic with worry. The findings showed that she had had an undiagnosed strep infection probably due to Scarlet Fever (not measles). The strep had entered the bloodstream causing septicemia[34] and settled in the clavicle as osteomyelitis[35]. It could possibly need an operation. She needed to stay in the hospital for several weeks on antibiotics. She could have come home sooner but she resisted taking pills or liquid meds. She'd take it and then spit it out in the sink. They had to threaten her with "shots". Carol stayed up in San Francisco alone as George had to go back to work in the Air Force. He could only get up to visit on his days off and it was a 2 ½ hour drive from Merced to San Francisco.

The treatment finally cleared up the infection, but it was a scary time for us all awaiting the outcome. Meanwhile, Kris had

---

[34] Sepsis; clinical name for blood poisoning by bacteria according to John Hopkins Medicine.
[35] Serious infection of the bone according to the National Institute of Health.

Lady Slippers

been undergoing periodic testing since birth for signs of retinoblastoma, her sister's fatal illness. Since there is a genetic component to the disease, Carol and George were screened for it. Occasionally, a tumor like this can develop when someone is a child and heal on its own. Scars would show up on the retina. Neither Carol nor George showed any evidence of this in themselves, and no one knew of anything in either's family background. They did recommend that any subsequent children be screened and that our siblings' children and any grandchildren watched also.

    Paul and Heather had their first child after they were married for five years. He was named Eric Joseph. After my mother died in 1973, the house in Travis came into my possession. Neither Henry nor I wanted to move into it, but when I offered to rent it to Heather and Paul with the option to buy, they jumped at the chance. Heather stayed at home to take care of Eric.

CHAPTER 12

Florida & Europe

*Back left, Henry, Steven, Dad (Raymond), David.
Front, Eric, Bernice, and Heather.*

During the in-between times, Henry and I took a trip to Disney World with Steven and David. Henry said I should try to meet my father while we were in Florida. He convinced me that I should make the effort. I called my dad and we set up a place and a time to meet. Before we started home, we made a detour to Riviera Beach. I spent a few hours with my dad and he got to meet his two grandsons. My father was still taking fishing parties out every day. In Florida, they take three fishing parties out each day. Most times, the placed they fish are right off the shore by Palm Beach. So, they are ready to fish after 15 minutes of leaving the dock. The relationship with my father improved after this meeting. I had met his current wife; Evelyn and she seemed like a good person in her own way. We got along.

On one of my visits, I decided to go to the tip of Florida. The day I picked out to drive there, Evelyn got sick and couldn't go with me. I proceeded on my way alone. It was a long drive but interesting. The great swamp was on my right side. It would have been nice to drive across that but time prevented me from tackling that adventure. Once I got to the highway to the Florida Keys, I tried to keep track of how many bridges I passed over by writing them down with tally marks (I think there were 42). This is a hard job when you are driving at 50 miles an hour on a narrow road. You are literally driving over an ocean. Some of the islands were only dots of land. Others were larger with houses and stores perched on them in defiance of the ocean's power and might.

On the way down, I was passed by many motorcycles heading to Key West where there was a gathering taking place. The

Lady Slippers

riders looked fierce and threatening as they passed by. I stopped at several places where the bridges had been replaced after storms. The approaches and ramps were left intact where there is enough room. People can then pull off and fish or picnic. The water is so clear you can see the bottom.

After I had lunch, I followed Route 1 to its very end and put one foot in the Atlantic Ocean and one foot in the Caribbean Sea. Now I had truly been from Maine to the Keys on Route 1.

On one visit I made down there, Aunt Dot came down from Ormond Beach where she was living with her sister, Lillian and Henri. I wished that I had had a tape recorder that day as they transported us all to Connecticut when they were young kids and lived in a totally different world. Cars were just becoming a way of transportation during their youth. They went from horse and buggy to cars; from winding dirt lanes to concrete highways in a span of 50 years. It was an amazing age as changes occurred in every part of their lives. When they were kids, everyone had an outhouse. There was no running water or electricity in their homes. Kerosene lamps supplied light. Most businesses closed at night. Few people had radios to learn about what was happening in the world around them. As mentioned earlier, washing clothes was an all day affair involving hauling water by buckets, boiling clothes, scrubbing them on a washboard, rinsing them and hanging them up with clothespins (my youngest grandson doesn't even know what a clothespin is.) Then the clothes had to be ironed because there was no wash and wear material. Even underwear was ironed to get the wrinkles out. Ironing clothes was the worst as the ladies' and some of the men's clothes had ruffles on them, each of which must be ironed separately. The iron used was a triangular piece of metal with a handle on it. It got put on the stove to get it hot enough to press the wrinkles out. Usually you had two irons, one on the stove and the other in use. People today don't realize how many inventions took place in the last century which drastically changed our lives.

Heather and Paul's next child came four years after Eric. She was named Amanda Jane. Meanwhile, about nine months after Eric arrived, Carol and George had had Jason Eric. He was an identical

Lady Slippers

twin that Carol carried for a full nine month. Jason was born first and the placenta ruptured, so his twin Michael was left without oxygen and was stillborn. Efforts to revive him were unsuccessful. Carol was huge carrying the two as they weighed over 15 pounds together. I went out to deal with this new sorrow and help with the baby and Kris.

When Jason was about 4 years old, George was sent to Okinawa, Japan for three years. I was going to visit them there but it was such a long trip (and expensive) that I thought better of it. Now that I look back on it, I regret not traveling to that part of the world. There were so many things we could have seen and the different lifestyle.

At home, Paul and Steven had attended Brooklyn College. Paul majored in chemistry and Steven in history. When David went there, he was enrolled in an experimental program which I thought was unusual. The class size was only about 15 students. A full professor taught each subject. There was no changing of classes. When you had Ancient History, all phases of the time period were covered – the geography, the jobs people had, the art of the period, the music, travel and politics. The Industrial Age was treated the same way. This program covered the first two years of the college curriculum. Then it had to be dropped because it became too expensive to continue, especially using full professors to teach. I think that if I were doing home schooling, as so many do now, I would try that method as it seems logical to me.

Steven got married at this time to Francine Riccio. There were married for seven years and then divorced. They had no children. Paul started working at Exxon right over the Goethals Bridge in Linden, New Jersey. He told Steven that the company was hiring so Steven took the test and got a job there also. Paul eventually became a Dock master there. He was called upon to clean up any spills the company made. He even went up to Alaska for three months to work on the Exxon Valdez spill[36]. For all of his years at Exxon, he was also in the Army reserves. While he was in

---

[36] March 24, 1989 oil tanker Exxon Valdez ran aground in Prince William Sound, spilling 11 million gallons of oil. One of the largest environmental disasters in U.S. History. Reference: https://darrp.noaa.gov/oil-spills/exxon-valdez

Lady Slippers

college, the ROTC[37] was canceled on campus because of all the bad feelings in the country over Vietnam. Paul enlisted as a private after he graduated from college. He kept getting promoted and finally became a Major in command of a Chemical Reserve Unit. Then Exxon sold out the company. The new company kept Paul and Steven in their employ.

 Dave was due to graduate in May, when Paul told him that the company was hiring in April. David passed the test, quit school, and went to work at Exxon also. Exxon started training the new people and then cut 30 of the newest ones. About 6 of these were hired back by Exxon on their Bayonne facility and David was one of them.

 After going through his breakup with Francine, Steven met Sue at work at Exxon and they were married. David also married and was divorced three months later. Later he met Liz and married her. This is the period when my youngest grandchildren arrived.

---

[37] The Reserve Officers Training Corps is a college program that pays your tuition while training to become an Army Officer according to GoArmy.com

Before that though, Henry and I took two trips to Europe. Carol and George had been transferred from Okinawa to England for a three-year tour. Our first trip to Europe was an adventure. We didn't want to go overseas and spend our time in a Holiday Inn. We planned the trip with a book called "Europe on $10 a Day". First, we would fly into Paris, spend three days there in a Bed and Breakfast and explore the area. Then we'd take a train to Amsterdam where we would ferry over to England and meet up with Carol and George and spend two weeks with them.

Everything started off fine. We arrived in Paris, collected our luggage, and got on a bus to go to the other section of the airport. We had quite a bit of luggage as we were staying for three weeks. Just as the bus started up, two people next to me jumped off. I immediately started checking out my numerous bags and to my horror, found out that my pocketbook was missing. Henry checked the things he had with him, and it wasn't there either. We had to finish the ride to the other section of the airport and then come back. We searched the area in the airport, but it wasn't there! I now was in

Lady Slippers

a foreign country with no passport, no ID at all, no medical coverage, and no return trip air tickets! We also were unable to speak or understand the French language. We had to get an official of the airline to come to the counter. He took us to the police station at the airport, acted as an interpreter, and helped us fill out paperwork. The police told us to go to the American Embassy in Paris to renew the passport and get the Traveler's Checks replaced. The airline official then called a cab for us and told the driver to take us to the Embassy.

Once at the Embassy, Henry was told to take the suitcase and go stand across the street at the entrance of the park. They – the US Marines – would not allow him to enter the Embassy with the suitcases! I thought there was going to be an explosion right there and then. Henry was fuming. I had my fingers crossed that he wouldn't blow up and get carted off to jail leaving me alone with no one to identify me in all of France. After getting into the Embassy, I then found out that no one works past two o'clock on a Friday in France. Everybody is off for a weekend in the country. I was told to come back on Monday morning!! Next, it was a block's walk to the

Traveler's Checks Office. They replaced my checks without a problem. We left there feeling a little better. However, our problems were not over. We had planned to stay in a Bed and Breakfast near the University, but we were on the wrong side of the river. The hotels on this side of the river were filled with people from the countryside who were spending the weekend in Paris. Also, it was hot, we were upset, the suitcases were heavy, and we were feeling desperate. We heard two people speaking English – a welcome sound. We asked them where they were staying and took a cab there. They didn't have space but made some phone calls to the other side of the river. At last, we had a place to rest and cool off but then there was another problem. The keys to my suitcase were in my pocketbook. Have you ever tried to open a Samsonite suitcase without a key? We had to borrow tools from the management to pry open the luggage. The luggage was now useless and had to be disposed of. There is nothing like a beautiful summer day in Paris when everything seems to go wrong.

Lady Slippers

Needless to say, Henry and I spent the evening not talking to each other. My careful plans for this trip abroad were in disarray. The following morning, we regained our composure. We took a guided bus tour of the city, as we had planned, and noted further places we wanted to explore. We took a boat ride on the Seine riding underneath its many bridges. People were fishing in the river or sunning themselves on the river's banks. We were amazed to find that Paris has a siesta time in the middle of the day. We knew that Spain, Italy, and Portugal took this time out but didn't expect that custom in France. We strolled over the cobblestone streets. We found our way around town on the subways. When you entered the stations, you were faced with a large map of the system. You pushed a button showing where you wanted to travel and the whole route was lit up for you. It showed where to go and where to change trains. It seemed very easy. We traveled to the Palace of Versailles in this manner. It took us quite a while to travel through this majestic building. We attached ourselves to a group that was being escorted by a guide. Thus, we had an escorted trip and learned more of the history of each palace room and of the gardens which surrounded it.

We visited an outdoor market in this city. We didn't like the way the meat was displayed in the open air without the benefit of refrigeration. We found that all the restaurants were closed. We asked some children on the street about eating. Their answer, "Do you have money? It's no problem!" They took us to a restaurant. It seems they do not open until 6PM. This is so different from New York where you can eat any time of the day or night.

We went up to the Eiffel Tower after dark. It was nice up there where you could look out over the lighted city. They have a device that lifts you up in a circle so you can look out over all of the city from an angle. We also attended a High Mass in Notre Dame Cathedral. It was an impressive building with so many buttresses and towers. The stained-glass windows were beautiful as well, a feast for the eyes.

We actually enjoyed the time we spent in the city notwithstanding the beginning few hours. Our hotel manager had a

Lady Slippers

lot to do with turning our trip around. He spoke five languages and could change from one to another in the blink of an eye. He took the time to explain and advise us and was an excellent ambassador for Paris.

Monday morning found us back at the Embassy to get my passport replaced. It didn't take long once we arrived with a new picture of me to put in it. We returned to the hotel to pick up luggage and be on our way. The manager said, "Let me call the airport again. Maybe your pocketbook is there." We were told that "Lost and Found" at the airport did have a pocketbook. The description of it sounded like mine. So, we took a taxi there and it *was* mine. Amazingly, all of my belongings were intact – not one thing was missing! The explanation was that someone had taken my bag by mistake. It was turned in right away. However, the "Lost and Found" Office is closed on weekends. Now I had two passports! The plane tickets were there so that worry was eliminated. We were able to take a train that afternoon for the next phase of our three week trip unburdened by Friday's events and with mostly happy memories of Paris days.

It was Monday afternoon as we enjoyed our train trip across the French countryside during the daylight hours. We arrived in town Amsterdam close to midnight. We wandered from the station into town and booked a room in one of the first hotels we came to. In the morning, when we came down to breakfast and looked out onto the nearby streets, we couldn't wait to pack our luggage and move out. This hotel was right in the middle of the famous Red Light District. The women displayed themselves in the windows for all to see and beckoned us to enter.

We quickly found another place to stay. This was an older building marked by a very narrow frontage area. The staircase was hardly wide enough for our feet and curved very sharply. We were a little apprehensive in this building, as it would be very hard to evacuate if a fire broke out. The encouraging point was that the building had survived wars, bombings, and floods over the many years that it had been there. It leaned a little to one side, but we found that to be normal in this city. The canals did not smell very nice as they were used as sewers by most of the houses. They opened the dams every so often to flush them out to the sea.

We found that the part of Amsterdam near the train station was a very dirty, noisy place, but after taking the trolley away from there, it was a pretty place to be in. The people were friendly and helpful. The fact that the city was below sea level didn't intrude into our consciousness during our stay there. Henry talked to the fire house personnel in most of the towns we stayed in. In Amsterdam their main job seemed to be pulling cars out of the canals. You can see why when you look at them. There are only curbs on the sides of the street and no fences or walls. Paris didn't seem to have many fires either. All of the fire fighters liked Henry's FDNY fire cap. He did give some away and he could have sold a case full of them.

We later went to the Zuider Zee to see the windmills but found that they exist mostly in pictures nowadays. We did get to see people harvesting eels. We are used to seeing much bigger eels in this country. My grandfather used to spear the ones in Long Island

Sound so I judged the size of those he caught against these short skinny Dutch eels. We wandered around and found out that there was a "Floriade" in progress. These are held every ten years to promote the sale of the Dutch tulips and other flowers. It took us all day to explore this beautiful exhibition. They had thousands of dahlias growing in one plot. They were all sizes and colors from very small to the size of dinner plates. Another section had chrysanthemums from button size to huge blossoms. Most of us only see the yellow or white ones here but they come in many colors. It was fantastic to wander down one lane of color to another lane, flower after flower. It was just like being inside a catalog with perfect blooms. It was a totally unexpected experience.

      The last day of our trip in Europe, we took a train ride into Germany. We left early and ran into an immediate roadblock! People were erupting from the station and jumping on bicycles which were left there every day. They then rode the bikes to their jobs in the city. It was weird to see people dressed in suits and dresses hiking up their skirts or pants legs and riding off onto the city streets.

Lady Slippers

We planned to travel as far as Cologne. We struck up a conversation with a passenger on the train and asked him about finding the cathedral once we got to the station. He sort of laughed and said we should get off the train and look. It turned out that it was right next to the station. We knew that the airmen had bombed the bridge right there and it was destroyed for the remainder of the war. We marveled at the fact that the church was left standing at all. They called it "precision" bombing. The church sustained a little damage from many fragments of the bridge which still hadn't been repaired when we were there.

Once again, we were in the right place at the right time. Europeans were celebrating their ethnic heritages. Many of the countries had huge amounts of people in their colorful costumes performing folk dances on the open courtyard in front of the cathedral. It was a marvelous pageant that we watched with enjoyment. In between the dances, we had time to find out that when repairs had been done to the church's foundation, many objects from ancient times were found to have been buried there. There were also the remains of a wall that was built for protection in the year 1000. It was another eventful day highlighted by the unexpected exhibition.

The train ride back to Amsterdam was without incident. We left there the next morning on the huge ferry that carries cars and passengers across the Channel to England to start our two weeks in the countryside and in London.

Carol and George met us at the train station in London. Driving and riding on the other side of the road takes some getting used to. The motorways have round-abouts in the centers instead of off ramps. Sometimes if you miss your exit, you can go around the circle until you get it right. It took about two hours to get to their housing area at RAF Chelveston-cum-Caldecott.

The English countryside was beautiful. Properties were separated by hedge rows. These were growths that were planted close together and were extremely difficult to pass through. The towns were filled with small houses. Some had thatched roofs with intricately styled designs. We watched the thatchers working on this in several locations. It takes a long time to do but it lasts for 100 years if it is done correctly. The houses in the small towns are built right on the sidewalks. Some of the panes of glass have waves or flaws in them or are mullioned glass. These were made by hand many years ago.

One of the problems in shopping in these small towns is that you have to bring your own boxes or bags (or you can buy them). Stores do not supply bags for free. The schoolboys wear shorts even on the coldest days. Their knees looked all red and frozen. The streets outside of the town were narrow country lanes with no sidewalks which made it difficult to walk along or to ride a bike.

We went to a nearby museum one day. It was filled with information about the canal system throughout England. Some people rent a boat and travel the canals on their vacations. They are given keys to the locks and maps. They can spend weeks floating over the countryside without worrying about traffic on the highways or the high price of petrol. You can cook and sleep on board or pull up to a pub for a meal and a pint. It seems like a relaxing way to travel.

We were told that the canals were lined with clay so the water would not leak out. To make sure that the clay was tightly packed, men would put on huge heavy boots and literally stomp the clay into the bed of the canal. The mules were used to pull the boats along the tow paths until they came to a tunnel under a mountain. At that point, the men on the boat lay on their backs and used their feet to walk the boat through the tunnel to the other side where there was another pair of mules. There were some overhead bridges which carried the canal water over some of the valleys instead of using locks to raise and lower the boats.

Another day we went to Sherwood Forest where Robin Hood lived. We saw and climbed into the tree that was made famous in his story as a "message" oak. Unfortunately, there has been so much building in the area, that only a small area of Sherwood Forest has been preserved. It is also difficult to find as there are virtually no signposts.

Our next tour was the city of York. We went to its cathedral. The church had just been refurbished, with special care given to the

Lady Slippers

stained-glass windows. Lead is used to keep the glass in place. We learned that just after we had arrived back home, the church was struck by lightning[38]. The fire caused a lot of damage as the lead melted from the heat! It was a terrible blow and slowed up the restoration. The basement housed remains of earlier Roman buildings. York was a walled city and we were able to walk along a section of the ancient protective walls.

An interesting find was made here when a foundation for a new building uncovered the remains of a Viking Village. The whole underground village was preserved including some of the layers of earth. You toured it by taking an amusement park type ride through it. You rode along the ancient streets and saw the houses and figures of the inhabitants as they went about their daily lives. There was even a restroom complete with its odors. The remains of the vessels the Vikings had used to travel to England were pulled up onto the

---

[38] July 9th 1984 York Minster was struck by lightning around 2:30AM leading to one of the worst cathedral fires according to The York Press.

ground where the river had flowed. Many artifacts were still being recovered and were displayed at the end of the ride.

We traveled by train into London to explore the capital of England. In the Tower of London, we saw the "Crown Jewels" which are heavily guarded and the place where the kings and queens had their enemies beheaded. We visited the prison there and found the walls to be filled with "graffiti". Each had a number next to it. We found one named "Bailey" and its number. The guard said that prisoner had been accused of treason and subjected to torture on a rack which meant he was stretched. He later was exiled and ended up in Amsterdam. We don't know if he was a distant relative of my family or not.

We did some brass rubbings in some of London's famous buildings. We brought special paper and pens and placed them on the brass plaques and then rubbed the crayons back and forth until we had an image on our own scroll. Outside, London seemed to be a rather gloomy town. I understand that this is because of all the years of soot from coal burning from its many chimneys which settled onto

Lady Slippers

the buildings. Modern heating is less polluting, and many buildings have been scrubbed to restore the brighter colors.

On another occasion we visited Braintree, England. This is the town that my ancestor, Joseph Loomis, left from in the 1600s to come to America. He landed in the Massachusetts Bay Colony. It was a lovely town with flint walled churches but because we were there on a weekend, there was no way we could research any information about Joseph's relatives who remained in England.

On the day that we left England, there was adventure and turmoil again. We spent the night in London so we wouldn't have to travel so early in the morning. We went to the train station to take the train to the airport. We boarded the train and sat there. We were late getting to the airport, hurried to our gate, and found that our plane had not arrived from the states. We had to call Steven to alert him to the fact that we would not be arriving at JFK at the scheduled time. Finally, the plane arrived. We were boarded but found to our surprise that we were headed for Paris. Because the plane had arrived so late, it had not been cleaned after its flight and it had not been furnished with food and drink. This was to be done in Paris! When we arrived in Paris, we were herded into a large waiting area, where we milled around passing the time. We could not go into the main passenger area where there were shops and restaurants because we had already been through customs. It was very frustrating, and it seemed forever before they finished getting the flight ready for departure once more. The word "home" took on a new meaning, one of anticipation and longing for what was familiar and a bit more predictable.

    The problems with our first excursion to Europe did not prevent us from undertaking another one two years later. This time we traveled to Zurich, Switzerland. We found the countryside beautiful and the city of Zurich, enchanting. There were flowers everywhere in the city proper, so many, in fact, that they had a dedicated water brigade to keep them healthy. Every morning this cart would wend its way on the city streets and provide water to the plants.

Lady Slippers

We visited a beer garden one evening. The people had immense horns that had been used in the mountains. People in the audience were invited to try and sound one note on it. I did it and the prize was a bottle of wine to take back to the hotel. We sailed across one of the lakes, rode on their fabulous trains in the countryside, and took a vertical railway to the top of one of the mountains. There we threw snowballs at each other and marveled at the cows who were able to stay on the sides of the steep mountains while still grazing.

We visited a wood carving establishment where cuckoo clocks were made and went up another mountain on a ski lift. During the first part we were suspended over a carpet of wildflowers. At one point, we had to get off and then on to another section of the ride. This time we were supplied with heavy winter attire, and we needed it as it was quite cold at the higher elevation. We found the entire area we explored to be exceptionally clean and litter free. The school children were taken on these trains also. They would disembark and hike back to their towns – a good way to exercise and travel at the same time.

In the middle of Zurich, there was a shallow river. We spent time watching these large fish swimming freely. There were swans on most of the waterways. The people say quite a few of them die of lead poisoning from swallowing the lead fishing weights. The weighs get snagged and fall onto the bed of the river. The swans eat them, thinking they are stones, which they need to digest their food but the lead kills them instead.

We left Switzerland for Germany by train. The first town we visited was Munich. As we walked along the street in front of the municipal building, we noticed that many people were standing in the area or were seated nearby as though they were waiting for an event to happen any minute. We decided to join them in expectation (of just what we didn't have a clue). As the clock tolled the hour, we watched in awe as the entire building came alive with animated figures, all doing something different. A little further down the street there was a small park-like area with benches and a stage on which an oompah band was playing and people were dancing. They were happy to have spectators join them. It was a toe tapping interval during our traveling and it was free entertainment. We then ducked into a beer hall. There was more music, and it was fun to watch the waitresses handle six or more of those huge steins of beer at one time. Some beer sloshed over on them but that didn't deter them one bit. Everyone was out to have a good time. You could sit there all night with one beer and watch and listen.

The next day we started a bus ride along what is called the Romantic Road. It was to take us from Munich to Wiesbaden. The bus traveled on the Autobahn at 100 miles an hour. The front passengers had seat belts. The rest just prayed a lot. We found that the cities seem to be surrounded by an area of "weekend" yards. People had gardens there with little pools for the children and tables and chairs on which to pass the time and their own picnic areas. Then there would be farmland, a small forested area, farmland, a picnic area and then the next city. People also grew vegetables along the train track right of way.

We stopped at one town which was an ancient walled village. It was from the year 1000. Inside, it was composed of narrow passageways with cobblestones that paved the area, surrounded by stone fortifications. This place was now being used for senior citizens who had a ten o'clock curfew. The gate was closed and locked at ten. No one told us exactly what happened if you got locked out, but it was not really near any other place either, so I guess you made sure you were home on time.

At Wiesbaden, we tried looking up Henry's relatives as this was the town his family came from. However, after one look in the phone book we decided to pass on that job, as it would take a week to call all the numbers listed under Dietrich. His sister, Leah, may have been able to narrow it down a bit for she had lived there for a few years with her mother and father. In fact, she had started school there. They, Max and Stefania, had moved back there in 1920 but then the government went bankrupt. They lost everything because the money was worthless. They had to struggle to get together enough money to board ship to come back here to the states and start again.

Lady Slippers

We next boarded a boat to float down the Rhine River as far as Bonn. It seems that every mountain top that we passed has a castle perched on the very top. It was a peaceful trip down the river at a much slower and relaxing pace than the bus ride. We ran into an interesting moment in Bonn. The motel didn't want to accept our Travel's Checks. We had to scrape together enough cash to pay for our room for the night. This left us with about $6 for our dinner. We ate in a McDonalds. We had never had that happen anywhere else in Europe. Maybe this time we looked suspicious or something. The next day we took the train to the coast. This time we crossed the Channel on the Hovercraft. That was a beautiful ride. The only problem for me was that I wasn't allowed to stand up in the front. You had to be strapped into your seat because you are actually flying like in a plane. This time we landed in Dover. It was spectacular to look up above you and see those white cliffs and be reminded of the song lyrics about this place.

We were back in England once more to visit with Carol, George, Kris and Jason. We learned that during WWII, England had turned every bit of farmland near London into airfields. Not many planes were kept at each field but there were so many of them! The barns were used as hangars for the planes. This way if one base got spotted by the Germans and bombed, not too many planes were lost. Besides London, the air bases ringed many other cities as well.

In Germany, the trains were fast, on time, and clean. In England, the trains were late, didn't come at all, and were dirty, especially the toilets. London's traffic was rather chaotic also. The subways seemed to be better run than the trains.

We regret that during our trips we didn't visit Vienna. We were so close when we were in Switzerland. It would have been just a mountain away. But we didn't want to leave Switzerland either, as it was such a delightful place to be and had so many things to show us.

We came home once more tired and happy with all the memories we got to store up. Every so often we can sit down and open our minds and replay the scenes that are stored there like a tape ready to watch again and we experience the trip once more.

CHAPTER 13

A Tornado & Horses

After George's tour of duty in England, he was stationed in upstate Michigan. It was on the eastern side above the thumb on Lake Huron. Henry and I visited them by car. We traveled up to Buffalo, crossed into Canada and proceeded across lower Canada until we crossed back into Michigan.

We traveled with George and Carol and the kids down to the town of Frankenmuth – A Christmas-all-year-long town. We had planned to do some more exploring there and have a leisurely dinner, but the weather suddenly turned ominous with high winds and greenish clouds. George felt that a tornado was coming and at that point he wanted to get us out of there as soon as possible. It wasn't encouraging when the radio station we were listening to went off the air! The sky kept getting darker and darker and the wind blew harder and harder. For a while the sand and dirt kept us from seeing the cars ahead of us. It took us about two hours to get out of that bad weather. It was the kind of driving where your knuckles turn white while you grip the wheel and everyone in the car keeps his mouth shut for fear of distracting the driver (or gets yelled at by him and everyone else). The next day we learned that the storm was a mini tornado. There had been numerous accidents and lots of wind damage. It was the kind of experience we all could have done without.

    We fished in Lake Huron but unsuccessfully on both occasions and we saw Tawas City where people set up ice shanties in the winter months and call it "Perchville". They drive their cars right out on the lake, chop holes in the ice, put up little huts with stoves for warmth and fish. Kris nearly drowned up there. George

Lady Slippers

and she were fishing for smelt in the early spring on the Ausable River and she fell right off the dock into the frigid water. Of course, she had heavy clothing on as it was still quite cold. George managed to reverse his net, allowing her to grab the handle and be hauled out. That ended that fishing expedition in a hurry. I did catch a catfish while up there – the one kind of fish I don't care to eat. That was in a brook near the lake. It was nice to see miles and miles of waterfront and beach area without anything on it. There are still many places in this country where people aren't. You can be totally alone. Of course, this was before the cell phone came along. Now that little ringy-dingy follows you wherever you go. People can't tolerate being in the wilderness – they have to stay "connected".

After two years in Michigan, George retired from the Air Force and returned to live in California. A few years later, Eric and I, Sue, Steve, and their daughter Rebecca, George and Carol, Kris and Jason, and their Japanese friends, Mayumi and Michiko, all met up in Reno. We had rented a cabin at Donner Lake. We then took off for Donner Pass where we stood below the monument that had been erected for the members of the Donner Party that had survived the blizzard which trapped them and their wagon train in the mountains. It originally had been one of the best equipped trains that had gone west to California. They had many supplies with them and also had several extra animals but to no avail. They had followed faulty advice on a new shortcut and wore themselves out blazing a trail over earlier mountains. They arrived at the Sierras too late in the season to cross and it was an unusually hard winter. The stock died, the ground was covered with ice and snow, and food couldn't be found. The camp was practically on Donner Lake which was filled with fish, but it was frozen solid and hidden under the snow pack. The monument base showed the height of the snow back then and you could easily visualize the situation. Many attempts were made to cross the mountains and seek help at ranches on the other side but those who tried were unable to reach safety. When help was finally found, the returning rescuers found very few survivors.

     Above our cabin, was a road with several switchbacks and an area where people go to practice rock climbing. There we

Lady Slippers

discovered the train tracks that the Chinese workers had blasted through the mountains. The rails were built by Leland Stanford and connected Sacramento with the rest of the country. The Chinese were lowered from the tops of the mountain down to the right-of-way. They would then set up the dynamite charges, light the fuses, and then be pulled up before the charges blew. At least, that happened <u>most</u> of the time. But actually, there was little concern about safety and many Chinese died doing this work for little pay, little food, and very poor living conditions. Even though it was such a poor job, there were always more of them willing and eager to travel here in sinking and stinking ships. In fact, they fought for the jobs. These train tracks had tunnels that were covered with slanting roofs. This was to prevent rocks and snow and trees from falling onto the rails. We stood on the tracks and could feel the vibrations through the rails when a train was entering the pass.

    One day, we took a gondola ride up to the top of Squaw Valley[39]. It is a ski resort with an ice-skating rink at the top and a

---

[39] Now known as Olympic Valley. The Squaw Valley Resort now known as Palisades Tahoe according to Wikipedia

fantastic view of Lake Tahoe. It hosted the winter Olympics at one time[40].

We then tried our hand at horseback riding up and down the hills. Because of Eric's age (below 18) I had to sign a waiver for him in case he was thrown from the horse. I made the mistake of asking how they would get us out of there if we were injured and wasn't very happy with the answer. They would get a Medivac helicopter which would lift us out of there and into Reno or some other city with a hospital! Going downhill on a horse presents some problems. You have to hold onto the reins, hold onto the pommel in front of you and hold onto the back of the saddle so you don't sail over the horse's head. Going up the hill is the same problem only you start sliding backwards. And you get told "Let the horse know who is boss. Don't let him eat the grass as you are riding along." Of course, that horse knows who is boss the minute you climb up there and does pretty much what he wants to do all the way along the trail. It was another interesting day in the country.

---

[40] 1960

Lady Slippers

There are some casinos in Tahoe which we tried out. We didn't win anything. We went bike riding next to Donner Lake and fished in it from rowboats. We didn't catch anything in the lake except for sunburn. One other time, George took Eric out into the desert to look for quartz crystals and they captured two scorpions. He put them in separate aspirin bottles since they would kill each other if left together. Every time someone wanted to take a pill, he or she was afraid of opening the wrong bottle. By using an investment casting method, George planned to change them into silver and convert them into jewelry. Carol and George have been rockhounds for many years collecting fossils, minerals, and rocks that can be shaped and polished. They also make jewelry of varying types. They have won many awards at the County Fair over the years. They both teach people their hobby and show off their rocks at an annual club show in Turlock each year.

Eric and I left the group and went back to New York on our own. We had to change planes in Denver. We were loaded onto the plane. They then found something wrong with it and took everyone off. They divided up the passengers and put them all on other flights heading east. We were delayed about two hours.

Another fun trip for Henry and I, was a Cruise to Nowhere on the Queen Mary. We went with Sue and Steve for our anniversary. The ship sailed out of New York into the Atlantic Ocean. It makes a wide circle and comes back into the harbor. We gambled in the on-board casino, watched many of the shows, danced a bit and of course, ate our fill. You could have breakfast at three different places and lunch just about anywhere. There was a full course, dress up dinner and then there was a midnight snack.

I was in the pool one time when they started a game. They threw all kinds of fruit into the pool. You had to swim for the fruit, tuck it into your bathing suit, climb out and give it to someone standing there. The one who retrieved the most fruit won a prize. I got an honorable mention. It was a silver tray from the steamship line with the Queen Mary emblem on it. The one piece of fruit that I handed to the guy was a banana skin. He asked me where the rest of it was, so I reached under the leg of my bathing suit, scraped off the

Lady Slippers

mushy banana from my leg and handed it to him. He didn't expect THAT.

Henry and I also went on a cruise to Bermuda. I had been to Bermuda before in 1967 with Paul, Steven, and Dave but that time we flew there. Carol was there at the time to see her friend Myra and her husband, Val who was stationed there with the Air Force. Myra was pregnant with Karen then. In fact, it was there that Carol was introduced to George, who was also assigned to Kindley AFB, through Myra.

On this cruise, the ship was able to sail into St. George's Harbor because they came up with a new docking method. Now there are engines that can move a ship sideways. St. George's harbor was not broad enough for the ship to turn around in. It had to anchor offshore and de-bark passengers using smaller boats. It takes a long time for passengers to do this. I was right up by the bow watching as we entered the opening to the harbor. It is called "the cut". It was a tight fit for a ship that large, but the pilot managed it nicely. We sailed right up to the dock and stopped moving forward. Then other engines took over and acted like a tugboat and nudged the ship into dock. It was a real neat job. We were able to explore all around St. George area. Then we went back to the ship, back into the ocean and around the island into Hamilton. I brought some of the pink sand home with me this time. The sand here is formed from coral reef that are ground into fine grains by wave action over the years. You can walk on this sand in bare feet as it does not get hot like our sandy beaches. Our sand has quartz particles in it and they attract and store the sun's heat. Here on Staten Island our sand is red in color while across the lower bay, in New Jersey it is white. It is also white at Coney Island and many of the beaches have iron particles which make them black. If you use a magnet on these sands, the pieces adhere to the magnet.

  A cruise is a nice way to vacation. It is a traveling city and activities are planned for you. You can gamble at their casino or dance to different kinds of music at the different ball rooms. You can swim at their several pools, inside or outside. You can play bingo or other games. If you prefer to be a watcher, there are many lounges or

Lady Slippers

outside chairs where you can put up your feet and just watch. There are movies and live entertainment. Every night while you are asleep, a schedule for the next day's activities arrives at your door. There are also full spas where you can work out and beauty parlors that can make you beautiful in an hour's time. You can go shopping in their many fine stores. And of course, you can eat and eat and eat. There is a full barbecue under the moon, breakfast at dawn on the afterdeck, a snack on the way from one place to another or meals in your room.

The shower in your cabin is an experience in itself. I don't know how heavier people manage it at all. It seemed easier to get wet, step out of the shower stall, soap yourself up all over then step back into the stall and rinse off! It is the same with the toilet. You'd use it and then stand away from it before you flushed it as the contents get blasted out.

Because of the size of the liner you are on, you had better have a keen sense of direction at all times. Once inside of it, it became impossible to tell which way led to the elevator or stairs.

Carrying a map on the ship was advisable as was marking your cabin on it with a bright star.

CHAPTER 14

Seniors & Grandchildren

At about this time, I joined the Blessed Sacrament Seniors. I took on the job of arranging day trips to the many dinner theatres within a day's ride, including jaunts to Atlantic City. This led to us trying overnight adventures of three and four days' duration. We got to visit many places on each of the tours. We had guides who directed us as to what we should look for and told us the local history. In this manner, we explored Montreal and Quebec. The day we were to tour Montreal, it poured so we toured the subway station there instead. It was nice and dry and clean. There were many stores there where we window shopped. We did visit the cathedral (Marie-Reine-du-Monde) with its altar and surrounding areas that are gilded with gold. Many miracles have been performed there and canes, walkers, and crutches have been left behind as a testimony to the cure.

In Quebec we toured the battleground of the French and Indian War. We saw where the British climbed the narrow lanes to reach the plain above and confounded the French who felt protected by the steep cliffs adjacent to the St. Lawrence River. They were not on watch against a vertical attack.

We also visited the famous cathedral of Notre Dame de Cup. There is a bridge there across a small lake in the form of rosary beads. When the planning for building of the cathedral was being done, the St. Lawrence River was between the building site and the marble and other supplies they needed. People started praying the rosary every day asking the Lord that the river would freeze over. It did and stayed frozen for five full days. All of the supplies could be taken across the ice which saved money and time. Many miracles occurred at this shrine also and crutches and wheelchairs remain behind to testify to these events.

We then went on a Thousand Island Tour and visited Ottawa. While on the St. Lawrence River we stopped at Hardt Island for a tour. This island was re-shaped into a heart shaped island. It

Lady Slippers

belonged to George C. Boldt, who owned the Waldorf Astoria Hotel in NYC, Rhineland Castle and the Bellevue Stratford in Philadelphia. This gentleman wanted to build a beautiful home as an anniversary surprise to his wife. It was to have an elevator, an indoor pool, and chandeliers made abroad. It also had a playhouse for their two children with a stage, where plays could be performed, and a bowling alley. Unfortunately, his wife became ill and died. Boldt was so heartbroken, he abandoned the buildings and they fell into ruins. People in the area also ransacked the place and stripped it of anything that could be used or sold. After many years, the property passed to the state of New York. As money becomes available, the building will be refinished. However, it will be a very slow and expensive job.

Our group has also visited Baltimore, Washington D.C., Annapolis, Myrtle Beach, North Carolina, Quebec and Montreal, Canada.

Another trip for the seniors was a special four car tour in which I organized. It showed some of the new and old attractions on

Staten Island which many of them had never seen. One was to Snug Harbor to the Chinese Scholar's Garden. You must go with a tour guide as the placement of many of the rocks, bridges and other landscaping features have special meanings. There is a beautiful moon gate, and many people like to have wedding pictures taken there. The buildings leading to the gardens have been restored by the high schools' carpentry students. This helps the students with on-the-job training. From Snug Harbor, we proceeded to Jersey Street and the Terrace and turned into the Staten Island Yankees parking lot. The waterfront has been transformed into a park and bicycling area. The view of New York Harbor is unimpeded at this point. Here, Staten Island has placed its own memorial for 9/11.

The next milestone was at the end of Victory Blvd in Tompkinsville. There is a marker in the sidewalk by the park that tells you it is the "watering place". All of the sailing ships coming into New York Harbor used to anchor offshore and refill their water barrels with fresh water after spending 3 or 4 months on their sea voyage.

Lady Slippers

Proceeding on Bay Street towards Fort Wadsworth, we went to the north end of Hylan Blvd. On this waterfront, we watched as the many cruise ships left the harbor on the way to Bermuda, the Caribbean, Canada, and Europe. This is also the site of the Alice Austin House. She was a famous photographer, and her house has been preserved and outfitted as a museum. You can also see the Coast Guard station toward the Verrazzano Bridge. At one time, all the ships entering the harbor had to anchor right there in the channel. The Coast Guard personnel would board the ships for inspection and the passengers were examined by doctors. If these people had infectious diseases, they were denied access to the United States and were put in a nearby hospital under quarantine. Many people died in that hospital. At one time, the people of Staten Island rebelled against this practice as they believed they were being contaminated by these diseases. They burnt the hospital to the ground[41]. The government then built an artificial island in lower New York Bay off

---

[41] According to Wikipedia this was referred to as the Staten Island Quarantine War. In 1858 there was a series of attacks on New York Marine Hospital in Staten Island, also known as "the Quarantine"

of South Beach and put the hospital out there. This was long before the discovery of antibiotics and many places in Europe had various plagues such as Yellow Fever.

Our next stop was South Beach to see the Dolphin's Fountain, the new Vanderbilt Hall, and the restaurant on the rebuilt boardwalk. Further down is a fishing pier and a circle of flags. We saw that the pavilion has been rebuilt at the end of Hylan Blvd by the Conference House, which dates back to the Revolutionary War. Concerts are held here during the summer months.

South Beach has a bocce ball court and teams come from Brooklyn to play in tournaments. Many players and family members attend these outings and make an all-day affair out of it. There are also sand sculpture competitions with prizes. Everything used in the sculpture must come from the beach itself.

I am also involved in the Decker Avenue Association. They are a civic association that keeps after the politicians of Staten Island to ensure that they do things that need to be done in the neighborhood. We know the right phone numbers to call to look into

Lady Slippers

issues like teenagers gathering in the various parks, getting potholes fixed which wreck your car, and help in dealing with problems like speeding cars that are endangering the pedestrians on certain streets. We are not a big group but we continue to put constant pressure on the officials until they solve the problem and shut us up. It's the embodiment of the old saying, "The squeaky wheel gets the oil." Our group helps maintain the quality of life in the area and gives us the feeling that we can do something about solving community problems. Democracy only works when everyone in it has a say, good or bad. If you sit on your hands, the others get the say. It is an everlasting fight and one that should be everyone's concern. Every day is a battle that must be attended to. For instance, sometimes you bring food home from the store and it is spoiled. The easy thing to do is to throw it out and take a loss. That doesn't solve the problem. It is a chore to make another trip to the store to return the defective food and get you money back. If you and others do this, the store will get the message. They need to provide a good product because the customers will not accept a bad one. You are in control every time you fight for what is right and best for all of us.

I can just hear my son saying, "There she goes again! Writing letters of complaint or calling the manager in the restaurant about poor service." My senior group will agree with my actions. When we book an event, we expect to get what we pay for in the way of service, food, or entertainment. They have seen me confront managers in all sorts of places, including Radio City Music Hall (maybe I learned from my Aunt Dot.) I do praise places that go out of their way to come up with excellent food, service and entertainment like Hunterdon Hills Playhouse in New Jersey and PMS Tours of New Jersey who have given us many enjoyable trips over the years. The bus drivers from Bayshore Bus Company have also been excellent in getting to places on time, traveling safely through all kinds of weather and traffic with only one exception over many years. I notified the company about that driver whose attitude was very bad. Here again, in doing this job I learned a lot about people. There are those who react adversely when things go wrong

Lady Slippers

and those who are patient and understand the problems. You find out quickly who your real friends are and who will walk away from you.

I want to include some of my memories of my young grandchildren, as I call them. Melissa is the eldest, then Rebecca, Marc, and Jeff. Melissa spent a lot of time with me. Her Mom and Dave divorced when Melissa was quite young. Dave had custody of her on the weekends and that meant she stayed in our house with us.

Melissa wanted to play softball at the age of six, so I started taking her to practice and to games. I would pick her up for practice 2 or 3 times a week. After a while she transferred over here to the field at the end of the block. I became a fixture up at the field as I kept score for the team each time they played. When Marc and Jeff joined the same league, I kept score for them also. That was nice because I could sit out under the old cherry tree in the shade and put up runs for each game. Yes, this field has a cherry tree in the outfield near the first base line. The park department wanted it saved as it is well over 100 years old. There are special rules that cover this unusual case.

All these young grandchildren are into sports, so now in my old age I am attending softball, baseball and soccer games and school plays, and "Kid's Praise" plays which take place in a church, and which tell bible stories in song and dance. Sometimes the kids had solo roles or were in group dances and singing. It enabled them to face an audience and perform. They performed locally and in New Jersey locations and in Connecticut. It added a lot to their individual talents, most important of which was the ability to take direction and to interact with many other people. At the same time, being involved in their activities kept me active and interested in the children and the adults that met for all the practice sessions on Saturday mornings. My horizons widened as theirs did. They certainly kept me busy and entertained. Sometimes scheduling got interesting especially when there were two games in different places. Rebecca, Marc and Jeff all played in their school bands as well. One night they each had a concert at the same time. Steve went to one, Sue went to one and I went to the other!

Lady Slippers

For a while, Melissa was bowling every Saturday morning. I took her most of the time, as her mom and dad were working. Finally, in high school, a bus started taking them to the soccer games that were away from home. Sometimes, Dave and I would be at the field if it were a special game. I liked going to her soccer games because I could see the games and stay under the shade.

Marc and Jeff play at Miller Field which hasn't a tree at all so I can't watch them play very often. It is either too hot in the sun or too cold in the fall. The area is also crowded with cars and kids and games as there are several fields in the one place. It used to be a military airfield and it can be used for emergencies by planes heading for Newark, LaGuardia or JFK Airports. Other soccer fields are being built on Staten Island but the kids' Titan League uses Miller Field. Marc will be playing at Port Richmond High School this year, and Melissa will be playing softball at Kean University whenever their season starts. So, you can see, my schedule has been pretty full for the last 12 years with sports of all kinds. I also got to watch them all learn to ride bikes, swim, ice skate, roller blade, ride scooters and skateboards. It was like being reintroduced to my preteen years all over again. With Eric and Amanda, I ice-skated with them. With these young ones, I didn't. By this time, I was fearful of being knocked down and breaking a hip. Poor Missy got put on the ice all alone her first time. She taught herself and got so good at it, she could skate rings around Dave, her dad.

Being an avid New Jersey Devils fan, Melissa decided she wanted to be a goalie for an ice hockey team! She was devastated when we all told her "No way". The equipment necessary would cost $100 every season as she was growing so fast, it would be outgrown every few months. In addition, these teams travel to many locations to play their games and none of us could get her there all the time. Also at that time, girls in ice hockey were frowned upon.

My other 3 grandchildren, Rebecca, Marc, and Jeff learned to ice skate at this time. Their Mom and Dad (Steven) both skate so they took them along to nearby rinks in New Jersey. Eric and Amanda also learned to ice skate when they were younger. At one time, when all my children were young, there were many shallow

Lady Slippers

ponds on the island which froze quickly. Clove Lakes Park was also open for skating often but because more and more people wanted to skate, the Parks Department required thicker depths of ice before it would allow the ponds to open. It became less and less frequent that the ice was thick enough either at Clove Lakes or Willowbrook Pond. Skating had to be done at one of the two rinks on Staten Island.

Some of the other sports these younger ones played included karate, basketball for the boys, soccer for all of them, baseball for the boys and softball for Melissa. Melissa did get to be the goalie for her soccer team and loved it. The boys now compete in swim races at different private pools. Watching them race is a pleasant pastime for me.

Now[42] there are two great grandchildren as well living in California. These are Jason's children Breanna Lynn and Mallarie Renee. We all went through another heart break, when his son, Collin Michael, was stillborn a few years ago.

---

[42] 2007

CHAPTER 15

Life

Throughout my life, I have seen many amazing changes in my home of Staten Island. Henry and I grew up in a very rural place with farms dotting the landscape. There were woods and meadows to play in. We walked everywhere or rode our bikes freely on the streets. Springtime meant a search for violets to bring home to put in a glass of water. Even dandelions and buttercups and Queen Anne's lace found themselves clutched in our moist hands as a treasure to savor. The brooks ran free to be waded in and followed as they wandered down the hills and spilled into ponds. Most of our days were spent outside in unstructured play dictated by one's mood at the moment. At times, we chose cooking. Nothing surpassed the taste of a plain potato roasted in the ashes of a small wood fire, slightly burnt and sooty from the ashes and eaten with fingers. It could be washed down with hand-squeezed lemonade with melting ice cubes and shared with a friend. Christmas trees were searched for in the woods and you'd cut it down yourself on a cold afternoon. It would be dragged home and turned into a fairy tale beauty for Christmas morning using paper trains of many colors and angel napkins made by the children. We'd also add strung popcorn chains. In summer there were pears and cherries which you picked from your own trees and peaches too if you were lucky. You shared your fruit with your neighbors and they shared their vegetables with you.

These are just some random thoughts that pass through my mind. Some mornings as I awaken early, I find myself deep in a profound silence. There is not a bird song, not a car beeping in impatience, not even the whisper of a breeze to stir the curtains. The silence can also be found in certain places such as parks. At these times, it is hard to imagine that I live in a city with so many people rushing all over for fun and work, eating, driving and always in a hurry to do something new and exciting. Certainly, it is a place of contrast, with noise and quiet side by side, if you take the time to look and listen. Don't just pass by. Observe and revel in the place and time you are in.

Lady Slippers

One thing to notice is that in nature, all things are recycled. A tree falls, after many years of providing shade and perhaps fruit for all to enjoy. What happens to that tree? It is absorbed by the ground that it falls upon, providing minerals and food for other plants to grow and take its place. Rain falls from the sky creating ponds and lakes. Then the sun shines brightly on those ponds, lakes, and puddles. The water evaporates back into the clouds to provide rain for another day or place. It renews itself as do any fallen animals or birds. The matter that is in each one goes into new growth.

Examine a head of cabbage or an onion carefully. Some force within the seeds makes these vegetables turn into leaves so tightly jammed together that you have difficulty in getting them apart without breaking the leaves. A vine comes up and latches on to any upright it can reach, then twists around that upright and climbs as high as it can go.

New inventions also interest me. One is a navigator for your car. You inform the gadget where you want to go, and it tells and shows you the fastest and shortest route to get there. If you deviate from that route, it names the street you took instead, recalculates, and then reroutes you to your destination. Global Positional Satellites in the sky provide the information needed to do this. Talk about "Big Brother" watching your every move. And, of course, the cell phone nowadays that people cannot leave home without. They keep you in touch with everyone, all the time, day or night. They can even take pictures along the way, get you help whenever you need it and are a part of every kid's every day wear. It is a whole new world today but these memories and more will always remain with me.

Lady Slippers

EPILOGUE

by Melissa (Dietrich) Bini

My name is Melissa Bernice Bini (Dietrich is my maiden name) – I am named after Bernice or "Gram" as I call her. As mentioned, I am the oldest of her younger grandkids and the only child to her son David. *I added some family trees, at the beginning and end of the book, to aid the chaos.*

Gram finished writing her book in 2007 but it wasn't the end of her story, she would have another 15 years of adventures that I, and others, wanted to share.

I did go to Kean University and play softball. My senior year (2010) we won the school's first NJAC championship and Gram was there – in her basketball shorts and oversized sunhat. During this time, I was living with her. I had my own room – which she let me paint this terrible teal color and hang posters all over. I graduated Kean with honors and went on to work for one of those cell phone companies (Verizon) she loved so much – I say this sarcastically, fully embracing the irony.

My fondest childhood memories were in Staten Island with Gram. The dead end that was Eldridge Ave was a place of refuge as well as stability since my mother moved frequently. There – with Gram, Grandpa (Henry) and my Dad (David) it was quiet.

Going to "Grandma's" was always an adventure. Gram and I would often venture to a park, like Clove Lakes Park, where we would find clay to bring home and make landscapes or jewelry. We were usually outside as much as possible, she was barefoot quite often, even when she stole my Razr scooter. If it snowed, we found a dangerous hill – either in length on Todt Hill Road (where there's still no cell phone coverage by the way) or in speed. One hill we frequented had hay barrels at the end to keep the sledding children from going into traffic – it didn't always work.

We went crabbing, skipping stones while we waited and watched the boats pass by. Every so often you had to pull in the rope – which had a cage at the end – you had to pull fast otherwise the cage would re-open, losing whatever haul you had. Bringing the

Lady Slippers

crabs home meant cooking them – we would always boil the water and throw them in headfirst to limit the suffering. The feast would take place in the kitchen, over newspaper, a bowl of butter and a game of Battleship.

When it rained, we would do projects or go to the movies. I credit Gram for most of my over-the-top History and Science projects that knocked the pants off the competition due to the attention to detail. At the movies we loved comedy and sci-fi; we were thrilled each time they released a new Harry Potter as we completed the book series together. Other times we would take the trip down to Blockbuster or Palmer Video on Forest Ave to rent a movie for the night. Today, there's a Chase Bank where Palmer Video used to be – across the street from KFC and the bank where Gram was part of a hold up; another one of the many crazy stories she would tell me. The armed robber told everyone in the bank to get down – which she did – as luck would have it, he chose her teller. She noted his shaky hand and skin color which she reported to the police after the ordeal. She had cash on the counter under her wallet, but he was too nervous to notice, he took off at the sound of sirens.

A lot has changed on the island; the OTB (off track betting) down the street disappeared as did the Comic bookstore. Several gems remained; Egger's Ice Cream Parlor, Bennett's Bicycles and of course the parades. Gram and Dad painted a skully board (game played with bottle caps) and stick ball field for the neighborhood kids to play – this was before a surplus of cars filled the streets.

There weren't many rules at Grandma's. You came in when the streetlights were on, and you didn't touch her flower bed – which was full of colorful tulips as well as other flowers I could never remember the name of. It was also home to a large cactus that kept the tweezers quite busy. Years later Gram would fall into that cactus, butt first, that was a fun trip to the emergency room – poor nurse. I had a frequent flyer card to the ER as well but for the most part Gram's brown bottle of peroxide or Epson salts took care of most injuries.

Lady Slippers

Grandpa was quiet during those years. He kept himself busy collecting cans and scrap metal, which he would bring to these machines that sat outside Pathmark. Every so often you would catch him inside channel surfing, stopping at a baseball game for a moment or two before passing the remote. In Gram's hands this meant Jeopardy or Wheel of Fortune while reading Reader's Digest.

They both had cars then. Grandpa had a white Mercury Topaz and Gram had a maroon Saturn sedan – yes, I see the planet theme now. Both had manual windows, which I'm not sure if they were a choice or another attempt to resist technology. She was very adamant that EZPass was just a way for Big Brother to watch people. I don't know why the government would care about all her excursions to New Jersey to get cheaper gas and visit Jersey Gardens (a newer mall at the time in Jersey City) but she stuck to the toll booths.

Driving with Gram was like what I would imagine being on a double decker city tour bus would be – except she was the man with the microphone AND the driver which was terrifying to any passengers (usually just me). She would always point out what used to be throughout the island (yet here I am telling you about Palmer video being a Chase Bank). We hit a police blockade once, knocking off the passenger side mirror, during an unwarranted history of a cemetery. We stuck to walking for our next few adventures.

Lady Slippers

Carol

Mom didn't mention anything about the attack on 9/11. It was pretty emotional for all of us. Paul was in Long Island, NY, he could not get home as the bridges were closed. As an army reserve officer[43] and potential one star general if deployed in war time, he had state police escort ready if war was declared. Eric was at work, at a school district, in Coney Island (Brooklyn, NY). He was crossing the Verrazano Narrows Bridge when the second plane hit. Amanda was in DC for college, near where the Pentagon hit.

Cousin Judy was evacuated from the World Financial Center building, where she worked, directly across the street from the towers. She made the last ferry back to Staten Island that day. They took people on boats to New Jersey.

It bothered us so much since Dad was a firefighter and Uncle Sal had been a cop. Staten Island lost half of its firefighters that day.

---

[43] Paul was Commander of the 464th Chemical Brigade which commanded all the chemical, nuclear and biological defense forces on the Korean Peninsula.

Melissa

Throughout my lifetime, she, and Irene (her cousin) remained close. She had friends at church, where she was President of the Blessed Sacrament Seniors, and in the neighborhood – since she would literally talk to anyone. Family was blocks away or a short car ride.

Household wise – she had a washing machine now but for some reason a dryer didn't come along with it. Gram had a clothesline on the main floor, upstairs and in the basement (for days when it rained). Having the neighborhood kids in the backyard could quickly become embarrassing when your underwear is on full display.

Beyond the clothes, there was a garden, with blueberries, tomatoes, and a pear tree. Wildlife continued to be a burden as I would hear mutters about the squirrels; they would take 1 or 2 bites of a pear before dropping it to the ground.

Inside, Gram had a cockatiel (bird) named Kama (pronounced comma) which was short for Kamikaze because "she

Lady Slippers

crashed into things." For those who don't know, Kamikazes were part of the Japanese Special Attack Units in 1944, essentially military aviators who flew suicide attacks against allied naval vessels. The fact that she named her bird after this just goes to show her dry sense of humor.

Besides Kama there was the occasional ant who "didn't bite much". Gram loved dogs but Grandpa didn't seem open to getting another, and I can't blame him after the Lucky stories[44]. Yet, the dog Gram spoke about most was a black poodle named Jacques. She said he was the smartest, well-mannered dog – all the neighborhood kids loved him. I always sensed Gram wanted another dog.

In the kitchen we got used to smoke as Gram often forgot about whatever made its way into the oven. It was a good thing Grandpa was a fireman. Her fight against technology continued as she threw away a digital camera I gifted her – she thought when it died it was out of film, like her Kodiak disposables.

---

[44] Page 67

Post-graduation (mine - 2010), Gram must've gotten bored with the lack of sports to attend so started going to Devils hockey games with my Dad, at the Prudential Center in Newark, NJ. They became Season Ticket Holders; there, she had the opportunity to ride a Zamboni – which she did with light up Devils horns and all! We cheered her on as she attempted a shot from center ice and did an interview as the oldest Devils fan. She met her favorite player, Martin Brodeur (pictured), and proceeded to tell him about how she would ice skate on ponds. While the Devils were away, she watched from her couch, if they played poorly (which was common during this decade) she had a Devils bear she would put upside down.

Lady Slippers

Carol

In 2010, George and I visited. Steve, Sue, Paul, Heather, Eric, David, and Irene joined Mom (Bernice) and Dad (Henry) for dinner at Charlie Brown's. Dad likes the buffet there and everyone else can choose what they want.

I had Mom take a picture with me and the boys. We all had tee shirts I brought that said, "Mom Likes Me Best". She didn't notice until after what was on the shirts and then told us, "I love you ALL the same."

In 2011 we surprised them and brought Breanna and Mallarie for a visit to be there for their 70th Anniversary Party. All the family and some friends were there.

I went with George, Mom, and the girls to visit the Statue of Liberty, it was the 125th Anniversary, and then to Ellis Island where the Dietrich and Arnt (George's side) family names are engraved on the walls outside the buildings. Another day, we took the ferry to Manhattan. We saw a dress in a window that was made from newspapers and when we had lunch, the waiter spilled a glass of water down Mom's back. We finished the outing by going to the top of the Rockefeller Plaza, which offered a terrific view, if you don't mind heights.

Mom sent me this note after our visit: *"Can't find words to express feelings after spending the past days with you. All my aches and pains vanished for a while. Love you all so much, Mom & Dad"*

Lady Slippers

Melissa

On September 14, 2014, Grandpa (Henry) passed away at the age of 94 at Richmond University Medical Center surrounded by family. Gram was by his side the entire time. High School sweethearts for 73 years. A retired FDNY captain from Engine Co. 153 Stapleton. That night and the days that follow were the first I recall Gram being so quiet. I didn't like it. I can only recall pieces of the service, which included service members handing Gram a folded flag.

The family rallied around her during this time. Carol and George flew in from California to attend services and help clean up the house. While cleaning, George discovered a box of cash and uncashed War Bonds from WWII. The bank needed a specialist to come in and verify them.

Gram then did what she knew best, she traveled. This time across country on Amtrak (train), to California via the Lake Shore Limited and California Zephyr. She had flown across country before but never seen it from the ground, she stayed up at night to watch the different station stops. My Uncle Paul (her oldest son) went with her. Gram spoke highly about this trip for months, along with the history of the American railroad. Uncle Paul however, when I asked his point of view was a tad different...

Paul

3 days of hell. My kindle screen broke the first day, so I was without anything to do for two days. She locked herself in the bathroom and wanted me to get her out from outside. I had to get the conductor, since they have a master key. Every night she wanted fish for dinner even after they told her they did not have any. She kept talking to strangers in the scenic car and they could not escape because she blocked the aisle.

I escaped by plane leaving her with Carol.

Carol

While in California, she had dinner with Kris and her husband, Scott. I let her borrow a hat and we had a Red Hats lunch at Sizzlers (pictured page 235). The red hats were a nod to a poem by Jenny Joseph, called "Warning", see excerpt below:

When I am an old woman I shall wear purple

With a red hat which doesn't go, and doesn't suit me

The message was to have fun in old age and forget about what others think.

She spent Easter in Merced, CA, where she got to see her great grandkids, Breanna, Mallarie, and Bailey and grandson, Jason. We visited Yosemite for the day. There was still snow on the ground. Right near the road, a coyote dove in the snow after a mouse. "It was just like watching National Geographic" Mom said.

Lady Slippers

Melissa

In 2015 she stole the show as Flower Girl at my wedding. Her punch cards at the hospital continued as she had some ghastly falls. Including one that terrified the neighbors when she rang their doorbell face covered in blood from a recent faceplant to the sidewalk. Thankfully the entire street knew and loved Bernice. Even the mailman, who delivered the mail by walking in the side door as a way of checking up on her. A family member (Irene's daughter Patty) ordered her a bubble wrap jacket as a joke – she loved it!

Kaylan and Melissa's Wedding at Lake Mohawk in New Jersey in 2015. Back left: George, Dave, Marc, Steve, Eric, Mark, Bobby, Paul. Middle: Sue, Ashley, Carol, Bernice, Heather, Kaylan, Melissa, Rebecca, Daniel, Jeff. Front left: Emma, Amanda, Luke

My dad fortunately, still lived with her so she wasn't entirely alone. We got her a cell phone, which was completely useless because she never remembered it or charged it. It took months of explaining that her cell phone would work OUTSIDE the house. After the whole camera fiasco, we were confident a flip phone was all she could handle.

In 2015 Sue and Bernice took a trip to Nova Scotia. Visiting Peggy's Cove Lighthouse (pictured) and the Titanic cemetery.

Lady Slippers

When my wife and I were pregnant with our 2nd child, we asked Gram (and my Dad, since he lived with her), to watch our 1 year old Aussie-Pom (dog) named Hadley for a bit. Hadley was a ball of energy but always gentle around kittens we were fostering and around Gram. Gram was smitten. My Dad said "I don't think you're getting your dog back." The two of them became inseparable. Gram had a dog again.

In 2018, Gram became a Member of the Daughters of the American Revolution (DAR); an organization of women who have proven lineal descent from a patriot of the American Revolution. Her lineage has been traced back to Joseph Loomis, who came from Braintree, England on The Susan and Ellen ship in 1638 landing in Massachusetts. Loomis would then move to Connecticut, where he is listed as one of the founders of Windsor[45]. A descendent, Amasa Loomis, fought in the American Revolutionary War according to genealogy paperwork.

On June 10, 2019, Gram celebrated her 98 ½ birthday. Carol and George flew in, Carol had a cheesecake to mark it and the guy wrote "98 in half".

---

[45] https://windsorhistoricalsociety.org/founders-of-windsor-trades-professions/

Lady Slippers

Paul

I took her to a cardiologist as a follow up from her primary care doctor, he told her she was in good shape for her age and there was no reason to see him again. She then told him that he was the third cardiologist she had seen in her life, she outlived the previous two. The doctor was kind of taken aback.

After, she wanted to go to the bank and supermarket. I took her to Northfield bank where she took out about $300 in $20s, which she proceeded to tuck into her sweater pocket. I cautioned her to put them in her purse, but she ignored me. We drove to the supermarket on Forest Ave and pulled up to the door so she would not have to walk. She opened the door to get out and a gust of wind caught the sweater and of course most of the $20s went flying through the parking lot and out on Forest Ave.

She then yelled at me to jump out of the running car and to catch them. By the time I shut off the car and got out about 50% of them were gone with the wind. A couple of folks brought her one or two back, but she then proceeded to tell me how it was my fault, and I should have gotten out faster.

I looked pretty funny chasing wild $20s through traffic while being yelled at.

Lady Slippers

Melissa

In early 2020 the COVID-19 Pandemic hit the United States as well as the rest of the world, bringing everything to a sudden halt. Canceling the remainder of Devils games that season as everyone was told to shelter in place, avoid all non-essential travel etc. This was very hard for someone as social as Gram. She couldn't walk down the street without finding someone to talk to, but she was also one of the most vulnerable according to the CDC. Anyone over the age of 65 was.

Yet my Dad still had to work – oil being essential and all - leaving him with the burden of caution and guilt as he tried his best to avoid bringing home the virus to Gram. This would be the second pandemic she lived through, being born at the end of the 1918 Flu Pandemic.

In June, she used her medical alert necklace, after experiencing very high blood pressure. No visitors were allowed in the hospital due to COVID, fortunately my cousin's (Marc's) wife worked in the hospital and could maintain some level of communication. Gram left with a pacemaker.

Not being able to visit, I knew I had to do something. Even with Hadley, my Dad wasn't much entertainment as he worked 12 hour days and would often sleep during the days he had night shift. The solution? Well let's say Gram had to allow some technology into her life. At 99, we created a Facebook account for her in preparation to set up a Facebook Portal in her living room so she could video chat with the family. When it wasn't in use it defaulted to a digital photo frame of her kids, grandkids and great grandkids.

Technology 1, Gram 7,946 (made up points).

The pandemic did hinder her 100th birthday bash. Facebook yet again, came to the rescue as she received hundreds of birthday cards from friends, family and people that cared enough. Carol organized a box with *100 different things*, mostly candies – which, if you know Gram, she had a sweet tooth. In May, they had a make-up birthday party at The Staaten, which was a catering hall on Staten Island.

Lady Slippers

Birthday dinner in Staten Island. From left, Heather, Paul, David, Bernice, Steven and Sue.

After another hospital trip, it become clear the family needed to look at options to get her some assistance daily. A nursing home was out of the question in my opinion – while it may provide some socialization, I knew she wanted to be at home. Being overprotective of Gram I was concerned with the horror stories regarding elderly abuse in Nursing homes. Plus, you couldn't take a dog with you. Fortunately, a family friend stepped up named Sara.

Sara

I met Bernice in Fall 2021. She was 100 years old. A bright, bubbly little spitfire, this amazing lady was eons more alert, awake and active than I was in my mid-40s.

The first thing Bernice established was the pronunciation of her name. It was not BerNEEce. It was Bernice, with a soft i. Though she was a woman of limited height, very thin and a bit frail, I was still intimidated by her insistence on getting her name right. Thankfully I caught on quickly.

Bernice let me into her home and her life… the stories, the past, the history of Staten Island, her beautiful marriage and family, her heritage… there was so much she had to share and share she did.

We hung out a lot at home. Her couch was her bed and nest. Her dog, Hadley, was her bestie and permanent pillow. We talked for hours, the TV blaring in the background… Tamron Hall, Kelly & Ryan, The Price is Right, Golden Girls.

Going through the mail was my favorite and quite lengthy task. Bernice had donated to every charity from "Save the Whale" to

Lady Slippers

"Save the Paperclips." We donated again to some and not to others. I read the news to her: the Staten Island Advance and the Daily News. She subscribed to both loyally and made sure we put out tip envelopes weekly. She was very generous. She never forgot a week. And when it was time for Christmas and Easter cards, I wrote out the cards and envelopes as she recited dozens of addresses she knew by heart.

Eventually, Bernice trusted me enough to venture outside the house. I drive a Dodge Ram 1500 pickup truck, so I expected hesitance, fear and possibly refusal. How wrong I was. At 10 decades young, this babe hopped in the front passenger seat (I pushed her butt a bit) and bobbed around with me like a teenager.

We went everywhere: shopping, banking, lunching, troublemaking. She was my co-pilot. Tiny and thin, Bernice was my rock in that passenger seat.

Now, you have to remember that Bernice was born in 1920. She was proper. She did not curse. She did not say inappropriate things. She taught me a lot in that way. She was also a very cautious person who followed the rules. More people should be this way. Stop at the red light. Let people go when they need to turn left. Yield to pedestrians.

So, I am trying very hard to abide by the rules of the road. I don't want to be an offensive person or dangerous driver. I am on my best behavior. We are on Forest Avenue, a woman crosses the street at the crosswalk. She is a person of above average weight, and I had to stop short to avoid striking her with my vehicle. Surely, Bernice would scold me for driving too fast.

"Slow down" she said calmly.

"I'm sorry." I said ashamed.

"You know, if you hit her, you will dent your truck." Bernice said with a straight face. Seconds later she glanced over at me. We started laughing uncontrollably together.

OK. Now I get you, Bernice. I love you. And after that we were just buds.

One time we were both trying to get into my white Hyundai with great difficulty. We clicked the alarm button and pulled violently at the handles. When I looked inside and realized we were trying to bust into the wrong car, I grabbed her. We waddled away as quickly as her little legs would allow. Our quiet laughing as if we were almost criminals made it harder to walk.

There were Taco Bell Cinnabites, which my little snack-monster adored. Should we get a 2 pack or a 12 pack, scratching my head at the drive-through? "Get the 12, of course!" Bernice yelled from her co-pilot spot, her hand reaching into her NJ Devils wallet and pulling out a huge wad of cash. No price was too big for snacks! From Nutella to cookies to a Dunkin Donut Frappe smothered in whipped cream twice the size of her head, which she devoured, Bernice had the sweetest tooth on Staten Island.

There was the kiwi clean up in aisle 5 at Stop n Shop when Bernice knocked them over, the "good" junk stores she could spend hours in, the dancing in the living room, fishing her wallet and checkbook out of the garbage a few times, the mini-Christmas tree she had me place on the dining room table in September, and of course, our nature walks.

People would always ask Bernice her secret to living such a long, healthy life. She would always reply that she just remained active, never stopped moving. But I know that it was more than that. Bernice never stopped enjoying… whether it was her family, a funny movie, her dog or a butterfly flirting with her in the garden, Bernice was in tune with all things beautiful.

And that was her secret. While I and the world fumbled on our phones, stressed over the traffic, and looked at our watches with a tense sigh, Bernice was admiring the budding trees, the mischievous birds and literally stopping to touch and smell every flower.

Lady Slippers

Melissa

By 2022, there was a vaccine and Gram just about had it with being cooped up. She wanted out of the house as much as possible, even if it killed her (her words, not mine). She was back to hockey games and visiting family; including ours for most holidays since at this point most of the family was spread out beyond the comfort of Staten Island and New Jersey. Here in New Jersey, she hung with her new generation of great grandkids; my kids Bennett,

Christmas 2021; Kody, Bennett, Sawyer, and Bernice.

Sawyer, and Kody. Taking a few trips to Medieval Times where she somehow always caught the eye of a Knight.

Gram celebrated her 101st birthday at a New Jersey Devils game. She got upgraded seats and put on the stadium's big screen where 60,000 fans sang Happy Birthday.

If it wasn't clear already, Gram was a very independent, social, and stubborn person. She wanted to enjoy life and made it very clear that she did not want to be hooked up to machines – hearing about her Aunt Rene you can understand why.

The pandemic was finally ending or fading – whichever way you chose to look at it. Gram was planning for her 102nd birthday party, a make up for 100 and 101. Another opportunity to bring the family together.

In November 2022 her body had other plans. Gram was young and robotic at heart (thanks to a pacemaker), but the rest of her body had weathered 100+ years and was struggling to keep up. She had pneumonia and couldn't swallow correctly; she didn't want a feeding tube. This stamped her final punch card at the Hospital

Lady Slippers

where the doctors brought up the dreadful word "hospice". I profoundly fought for in-home hospice as I knew that's where she would want to be.

They attempted to bring her home twice but her oxygen levels would not cooperate. On December 10th, her birthday, they finally made it happen. Several family members were there to welcome her home, birthday balloons ready.

She turned 102 surrounded by loved ones, her dog Hadley and a nurse. She then fell asleep peacefully. Around 1am on December 11th (the day after her birthday), Hadley woke up my Dad to let him know. Part of me knows, if she were writing this she would say, "that's the way to go."

102 years of Bernice was not enough. She was a beautiful human being who fully embraced people and adventure. She inspired many, including myself. I hope her story inspires you too.

I re-titled this book "Lady Slippers" because Gram called them a treasure, hidden in Staten Island. I think that truly describes her; *a treasure hidden on Staten Island.* After reading her story, I made it a point to live more in the moment, to put the phone down. I went for a haircut, my first after Gram passed, and noticed the florist next door was called Ladyslipper Floral. I laughed and thought of Gram.

Bernice Dietrich & Melissa Bernice Bini

Lady Slippers

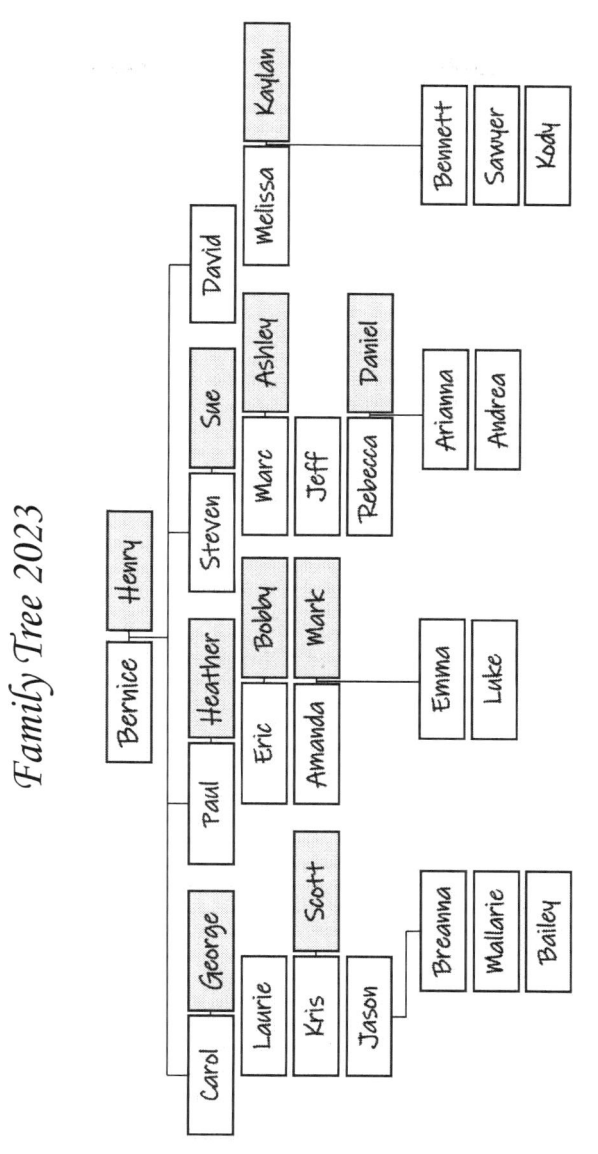

Family Tree 2023

- Carol
- George
  - Laurie
  - Kris
  - Scott
    - Jason
      - Breanna
      - Mallarie
      - Bailey
- Bernice — Henry
  - Paul
  - Heather
    - Eric
    - Bobby
    - Amanda — Mark
      - Emma
      - Luke
  - Steven — Sue
    - Marc
    - Ashley
      - Jeff
    - Rebecca — Daniel
      - Arianna
      - Andrea
  - David
    - Melissa — Kaylan
      - Bennett
      - Sawyer
      - Kody

*Limited to family members mentioned.